C000255912

EXPLORING SCIENCE 8

INTERNATIONAL 11-14

Mark Levesley, Sue Kearsey, Ian Bradley, Alice Jensen, Sarah Longshaw, Kat Day, Penny Johnson

WORKBOOK

P Pearson

CONTENTS

8Aa FOOD AND ADVERTISING

1 Why do we need to eat food? ....

....

2 Look at the food chain.

State the source of energy for:

a the swallow

....

b the oak tree.

....

oak tree   greenfly   ladybird   swallow

3 In your digestive system, food is taken into your body by the small intestine.

a Tick (✓) *all* the organs that are part of the digestive system.

☐ artery   ☐ bladder   ☐ brain   ☐ heart
☐ kidney   ☐ large intestine   ☐ oesophagus   ☐ pancreas
☐ skin   ☐ small intestine   ☐ spinal cord   ☐ stomach

b What carries digested substances from your small intestine to all the cells of your body? ....

4a Design a healthy meal plan for one day.

Breakfast: ....

....

Lunch: ....

....

Dinner: ....

....

b You will be given instructions for this question later!

....

....

8Aa NUTRIENTS

1 What do scientists mean by diet? ....

2 The table shows the nutritional information found on a packet of food.

a Draw a smile on the face in the box to show how confident you are in understanding the label – the bigger the smile, the more confident you are.

:·)	**Typical values**	**Per 100 g**	**Per 175 g portion**
	protein	2.0 g	3.5 g
	carbohydrate	9.2 g	16.1 g
	of which sugars	3.5 g	6.1 g
	fat	1.8 g	3.2 g
	of which saturates	0.3 g	0.5 g
	fibre	2.3 g	4.0 g

b How many grams of carbohydrate are in 100 g of

the food? ....

c How many grams of protein do 200 g of this food

contain? ....

d Calculate the grams of fat in two portions of the

food. ....

e Give the names of *two* nutrients *not* found in this food.

....

f What do we need nutrients for? Tick (✔) *all* the correct reasons.
- ☐ for growth
- ☐ for food
- ☐ for energy
- ☐ for repair
- ☐ for good flavour
- ☐ for our stomachs

g Some carbohydrates in the food are sugars. Name *one* sugar. ....

h Give *one* reason why you need to eat fibre.

....

3 Complete the table to show some tests for different nutrients.

Nutrient	Test	Positive result
	rub on paper	greasy mark
protein		turns from blue to purple
starch	iodine solution	

8Ab USES OF NUTRIENTS

1a Name *one* activity in which your body gains mass. _____

b Name *one* activity in which your body loses mass. _____

2 Why do you need starch in your diet? _____

3a What does your body use fat for? _____

_____

_____

_____

b State *one* food that is a good source of fat. _____

4 The table shows the amount of energy in some different foods.

a Give the unit symbol that is missing in the top row

of the table. _____

b Which food contains the most energy?

_____

Energy in different foods (_____)		
Typical values	**Per 100 g**	**Per portion**
banana	370	370
breakfast cereal	1530	360
milk	275	330

c State the mass of banana in *one* portion. _____

d Calculate the amount of energy in a portion of cereal served with a portion of milk and a portion of banana.

5 Which process releases energy from food? Tick (✔) *one* box.

☐ **A** respiration   ☐ **B** excretion   ☐ **C** digestion   ☐ **D** exhalation

6 Draw *one* line between each 'need' and a 'nutrient'. Draw another line between each 'nutrient' and a 'good source'.

Need	**Nutrient**	**Good source**
strong bones	carbohydrate	potatoes
for fuel	protein	carrots
healthy eyes	vitamin A	meat and eggs
growth and repair	calcium	milk

1 The table shows the energy required by different activities.

a Which activity requires the most energy?

Activity	Energy required per hour (kJ/h)
sleeping	180
watching TV	250
walking slowly	470
cycling slowly	660
running fast	1700

....

b Calculate the amount of energy used when you:

i walk slowly for 2 hours ....

ii cycle slowly for 3 hours ....

iii sleep for 2.5 hours. ....

c Look at both the tables on this page and the last. How many portions of milk provide enough energy for

1 hour of slow cycling? ....

d Hosni goes for a slow walk for 1 hour, and then watches TV. After 2 hours he falls asleep for 30 minutes. Calculate the energy he has used.

2a Ravi is a fitness trainer. His wife is the same age and works at a call centre. Who will need more energy

per day? ....

b Explain why this is. ....

....

3 Discuss in a group which of the following need more energy each day: teenagers or young children, who both have similar levels of activity. Write your answer below and why your group thinks this.

Who needs more energy: ....

Why we think this: ....

....

8AC BALANCED DIETS

1 In groups, discuss how the words on the left can be linked with the words on the right using a simple phrase. Then complete the lines with your best ideas. It may help to use different colours. One has been done for you.

protein		insulation
fat	is used by the body for	growth and repair
carbohydrate		carbohydrate
sucrose		energy
water		blood
scurvy		vitamin C

2 Complete the sentences using words from the box. Use each word once.

balanced	foods	malnutrition	nutrient	nutrients	variety

To stay healthy people should have a .... diet, which means that

they eat a wide .... of .... to give them

all the .... they need. People who have too much or too little of a

.... may suffer from ....

3a This diagram shows the amount of food that should come from different food groups in a healthy diet. Draw lines from the labels to complete the diagram. One has been done for you.

b Martin's diet consists mainly of French fries, lamb mince, white bread, low-fat spread and cola. He claims that his diet is healthy because he only uses low-fat spread. Explain why he is wrong.

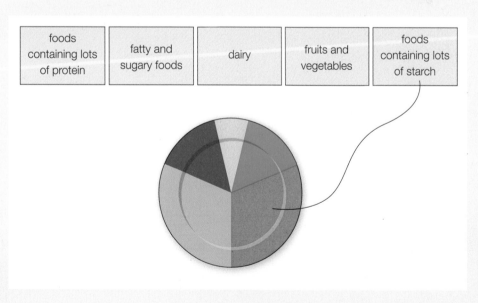

foods containing lots of protein | fatty and sugary foods | dairy | fruits and vegetables | foods containing lots of starch

....

....

....

SB

4 How will a balanced diet stop people becoming overweight?

....

....

5 Draw lines to match each deficiency disease with its cause and symptoms.

Deficiency disease	**Cause**	**Symptoms**
kwashiorkor	too little protein	poorly formed bones
night blindness	too little iron	poor vision in low light
rickets	too little vitamin A	tired and short of breath
anaemia	too little vitamin D	large belly

6a Which of these are problems often caused by obesity? Tick (✓) *all* the correct boxes.

☐ starvation ☐ being overweight ☐ high blood pressure
☐ heart disease ☐ scurvy ☐ low pulse rate

b People who are obese are more likely to suffer from a problem called angina, in which heart muscles do not get enough blood.

i Describe why the heart muscles do not get enough blood.

....

....

ii What happens to muscle cells if they do not get enough blood?

....

....

7 The reference intake for adults is 50 g of protein. Describe what this means.

....

....

8 Look at your answer to question **4a** on page 3. For part **b** explain why your meal plan is healthy or explain how you could improve it.

1 People have asked a pizza company to use healthier pizza bases. The nutrition information for the existing pizza base is shown.

a State some ways in which the pizza base could be made healthier.

....

....

....

b Choose *one* way and explain *two* ideas for changing the pizza base in this way.

....

....

....

....

Pizza base		
Ingredients		
Bleached white flour, water, glucose, sucrose, salt, hydrogenated vegetable oil (to add stretchiness), xanthan gum (to add stretchiness)		
Nutrition Information		
Typical values	**per 100 g**	**per serving** (¼ base)
Energy	1059 kJ	585 kJ
Protein	9 g	5 g
Carbohydrate	62 g	34 g
of which **sugars**	14 g	8 g
Fat	5 g	2.5 g
Fibre	0.2 g	0.1 g
Allergy advice Product contains gluten		

c Choose *one* idea and design a delivery box to advertise your new pizza base. Draw your design on the outline below.

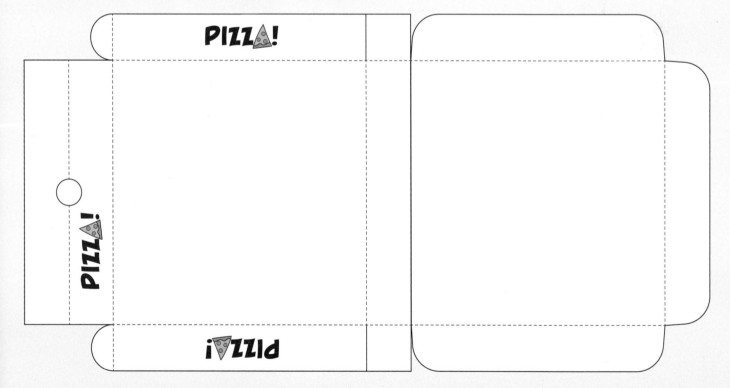

1 What is an organ system?

....

2a What does the digestive system do? ....

b Why do we need to digest food? ....

....

3 The liver makes a substance that helps digestion. List *three* other organs that also produce substances that help with digestion.

....

....

....

....

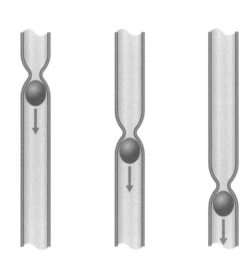

4 Work in a group to discuss how to add *two* or *three* short labels to the diagram to explain how food is moved down from the mouth. Then write in your labels.

5 Draw lines to link each part of the digestive system with its name and function.

Digestive system

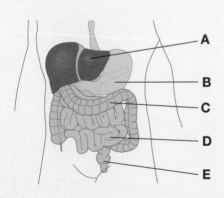

A

B

C

D

E

Organ name	Organ function
large intestine	food is mixed with acid and digestive juices
liver	food is digested and small molecules are absorbed
rectum	makes a substance to help digest fats
small intestine	stores faeces
stomach	water is removed from undigested food

6 Write the words from the box next to the correct meanings.

| absorption | defaecation | egestion | excretion | ingestion |

a .... getting rid of undigested food from your gut as faeces

b .... getting rid of undigested food from your gut as faeces

c .... eating food

d .... soluble molecules moving into the blood

e .... getting rid of waste substances produced in cells

7 Give *one* benefit and *one* disadvantage of having bacteria in your gut.

Benefit ....

Disadvantage ....

8 Describe how enzymes help digestion. ....

....

9a Enzymes are often called 'biological catalysts'. Discuss in a group why this might be. Write your answer below.

Enzymes are often called 'biological catalysts' because ....

....

....

b Compare your group's answer with another group. If you can, write down *one* way in which you could improve your answer.

....

....

10 Use the scissors model to explain how enzymes work.

....

....

....

1 Calculate the area of a basketball court, which is 28 m long and 15 m wide.

2a Calculate the surface area of the *smallest* face of the cuboid in the diagram.

b Calculate the surface area of the cuboid.

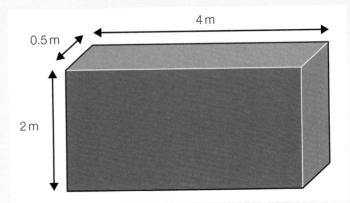

c Calculate the surface area : volume ratio of the cuboid. Give your answer as a decimal without units.

d The cuboid is chopped into 6 smaller cuboids. Cross out the incorrect words.

i The total surface area *increases / decreases / stays the same*.

ii The total surface area : volume ratio *increases / decreases / stays the same*.

3 Tick (✓) the phrase that *best* completes the following sentence.

To get enough of the substances they need from their surroundings, a cell needs:

- ☐ **A** a large volume compared to its surface area.
- ☐ **B** a large surface area compared to its volume.
- ☐ **C** a small surface area compared to its volume.
- ☐ **D** a surface area that is equal to its volume.

SB

4 Explain why the same amount of food is digested faster when it is in small pieces compared with large pieces.

5 Calculate the increase in the surface area : volume ratio of this cube when it is divided into smaller cubes, as shown.

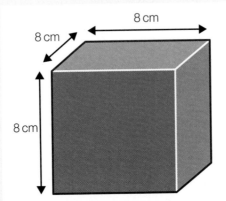
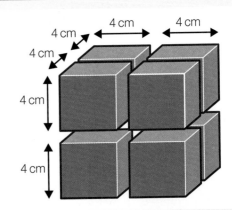

8Ae ABSORPTION

1 The diagram shows a model of the small intestine. Visking tubing is a thin material containing tiny holes that only small molecules can pass through.

a In the model, what does the Visking tubing represent?

....

b In the model, what does the water outside the tubing represent?

....

....

c What would you expect to find in the water at the end of the experiment shown in the diagram that was

not there at the start? Explain your reasoning. ....

....

....

Visking tubing

mixture of water, enzymes and starch

water

tightly tied

2 Explain why there is an overall movement of soluble molecules out of the small intestine. To answer this, tick (✓) *one* box for each of parts **a** and **b** below.

a The soluble molecules move by:
- ☐ **A** dissolving.
- ☐ **B** enzymes.
- ☐ **C** diffusion.
- ☐ **D** Brownian motion.

b This is because:
- ☐ **A** the soluble molecules are more concentrated inside the small intestine.
- ☐ **B** there is more water inside the small intestine.
- ☐ **C** there is more pressure inside the small intestine.
- ☐ **D** enzymes attach to the molecules.

3 How is the small intestine adapted to absorbing digested nutrients quickly?

....

....

....

....

8Ae PACKAGING AND THE LAW

1 Look at the nutrition label.

a List the nutrients shown on the label.

....

....

b Give the name of a carbohydrate that is *not* a sugar.

....

c How many grams of protein are there in two servings of this food?

....

....

d State what the body uses protein for. ....

e Explain why there is an orange band on the fat for this food. ....

....

....

Nutrition		
Typical values	100 g contains	Each serving (44 g) contains
Energy	1600 kJ	700 kJ
Fat	11 g	4.8 g
of which saturates	8 g	3.5 g
Carbohydrate	45.5 g	20.0 g
of which sugars	3.8 g	1.7 g
Fibre	2.8 g	1.2 g
Protein	7.7 g	3.4 g
Salt	1.0 g	0.4 g

2 Name a nutrient *not* on the nutrition label and describe its use in the body.

Name of nutrient ....

What it is used for ....

SB

3 Draw a flow chart to show how cells get a fuel for respiration after you have eaten starch.

4a In groups, discuss how to eat healthily. Record your group's ideas below.

....

....

b Compare your group's answer with another group. If you can, write down *one* way in which you could improve your answer.

....

....

8Ba USEFUL PLANTS

1 All plants are in the plant kingdom. Name *one* other kingdom.

....

2a Describe *one* way in which plants are used in each of the following.

i food ....

ii clothing ....

iii building ....

iv medicine ....

b Compare your answers with other students. Write the best example from their answers below.

i food ....

ii clothing ....

iii building ....

iv medicine ....

c Describe *one* other way in which we use plants.

....

3 Describe what happens when bees pollinate flowers.

....

....

4 Describe how pollination leads to seed formation in flowers.

....

....

5 Suggest *one* way in which plants spread their seeds.

....

....

8Ba CLASSIFICATION AND BIODIVERSITY

1a What characteristics of animals are different from those of plants?

b What are the other three kingdoms?

2 *Bellis perennis*, *Leucanthemum vulgare* and *Bellis sylvestris* are all flowering plants that are called daisies.

a Name *one* genus of daisies.

b Give *one* species name of daisies.

c Suggest which *two* of these species of daisies are most similar. Give a reason for your answer.

3 How are flowering plants and conifers:

a similar

b different?

4 Fungi were once thought to belong to the plant kingdom.
a Suggest why they were grouped with plants.

b Give *one* reason why they are no longer grouped with plants.

5a Tick (✓) *one* box in each row to show how these animals are classified.

Animal	Invertebrate	Vertebrate
snail	☐	☐
fish	☐	☐
snake	☐	☐
fly	☐	☐

b Give a reason for your answers to part **a**.

....

6 Draw *one* line from each animal group to its characteristics.

Animal group	**Characteristics**
mammals	hard-shelled eggs, feathers
amphibians	leathery-shelled eggs, dry scaly skin
birds	jelly-coated eggs, moist skin
reptiles	have hair; young fed on milk

7 Look at this drawing of an animal.

Is this animal a mollusc, an insect or an arachnid? Give a reason for your answer.

....

....

8a State what is meant by biodiversity.

....

b Discuss with a partner why biodiversity should be preserved. Write your best answer to this here.

....

....

....

1 Draw *one* line from each scientific term to its definition.

Scientific term

| accurate |
| estimate |
| sample |
| quadrat |

Definition

| a part taken from the whole for measurement |
| a measurement that is close to the real value |
| a square frame used to sample habitats |
| a measurement that is approximate |

SB

2 A sweet jar is 50 cm tall. Sweets are taken from the top 5 cm. There are 24 sweets. Estimate the total number of sweets in the jar. Show all your working.

3 Give *one* reason why scientists use samples to estimate the populations of organisms.

4a Describe how a quadrat is used to sample organisms in the environment.

b Explain why quadrats are placed randomly when estimating populations.

5 A field is a rectangle 20 m long by 15 m wide. A quadrat 0.5 m × 0.5 m was placed 10 times on the field. A total of 6 daisy plants were counted inside the quadrats.

a Estimate the daisy plant population in the whole field. Show your working.

SB

b Give *one* advantage and *one* disadvantage of placing the quadrat 20 times on the field instead of 10 times.

Advantage

Disadvantage

8Bb TYPES OF REPRODUCTION

1 Use words from the box to complete the text. You may use each word once, more than once or not at all.

| gamete | inherit | offspring | parent | zygote |

Sexual reproduction happens when a male _____ joins with a female

_____ to form a _____. The offspring will

_____ some characteristics of their male _____ and

some characteristics of their female _____.

2 The scientific name of the apricot is *Prunus armeniaca*, and the scientific name of the plum is *Prunus domestica*. A plumcot is produced by sexual reproduction of a plum and an apricot.

a Tick (✓) *one* box to show which term is used to describe a plumcot.
- ☐ **A** species
- ☐ **B** hybrid
- ☐ **C** fertile
- ☐ **D** asexual

b Discuss the following with a partner, then write down your agreed answers.

i How can you use their scientific names to determine how closely related the apricot and plum are?

_____

_____

ii Why can you *not* produce plumcot seeds through reproduction between *two* plumcot plants?

_____

_____

iii You can produce new plumcot plants by taking cuttings from a plumcot plant. Will the new plants show inherited variation? Give a reason for your answer.

_____

_____

3 What do strawberry plants use to reproduce:

a sexually _____

b asexually? _____

1a Use words from the box to label the reproductive parts of the flower.

| anther | carpel | filament | ovule | pistil | stamen | stigma | style |

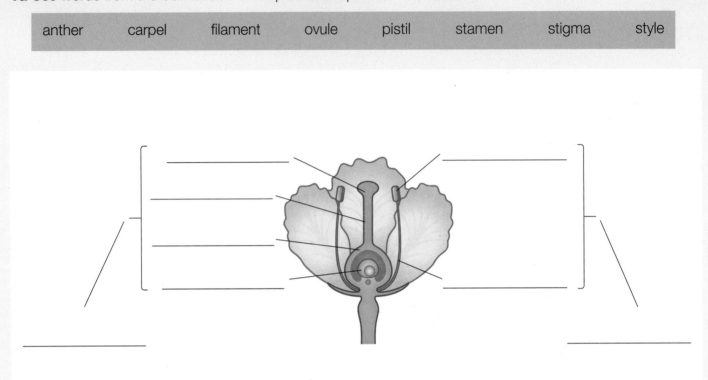

b State the function of the anther. ....

c Name the flower part in which the female gamete is found. ....

SB **d** Name the male reproductive organ in plants. ....

SB **2a** What happens in pollination?

....

....

....

b Explain why pollination is needed in plant sexual reproduction.

....

....

....

3a Complete the table to describe the characteristics of wind-pollinated and insect-pollinated flowers.

Characteristic	Wind-pollinated	Insect-pollinated
petals		
anther position		
stigma structure		
pollen grains		
scent		

b Compare your table with a partner. Write any better answers in the table in a different colour.

4 What is meant by cross-pollination?

....

....

5 A gardener plants some apple trees. One tree has flowers that only contain anthers, the other trees have flowers that only have stigmas. Explain the importance of the tree with anthers.

....

....

....

6 Explain why plants have ways of avoiding self-pollination.

....

....

SB

1 2000 cm³ of air is filtered through a machine. It traps 268 pollen grains. Calculate the concentration of pollen grains in grains/cm³.

2 In the activity, what hypothesis did you choose to test?

3 Describe how you controlled other variables in your investigation so that they affected the results as little as possible.

4a Write the details of where or when you placed each slide in the table below.

Details of slide	Rank order

b After looking at the slides with a microscope, rank the slides in order, with 1 being the slide with the most pollen.

5 Write a conclusion from your results about the conditions in which there is most pollen in the air.

6 Describe how you could estimate the number of pollen grains on one of your slides.

1a Number the statements in the order that describes what happens after pollination. The first one has been done for you.

I	A pollen grain sticks to the stigma.
	The male gamete joins the female gamete in the ovule.
	The male gamete moves down the pollen tube to the ovule.
	The nuclei of the gametes fuse to form a zygote.
	A tube grows from the grain down through the style to the ovule.

b Tick (✓) *one* box to name the process in which the male and female nuclei fuse.

☐ **A** pollination   ☐ **C** fertilisation
☐ **B** germination   ☐ **D** seed formation

2 What does the zygote go on to form? ....

3a Label the structures on the diagram of a bean seed.

b Which *two* structures on the diagram are parts of the embryo?

....

c Describe the functions of the other two structures labelled on the diagram.

....

....

d Which part of the flower develops into the fruit around a seed?

....

4 The fruits of some plants have 'wings' that make them spin as they fall. The table shows the results of an experiment to find out how the length of wings on a model spinner affects the time it takes to fall 2.5 m.

Length of wings (cm)	1st drop time (s)	2nd drop time (s)	3rd drop time (s)	Mean drop time (s)
10	2.63	2.66	2.57	
8	2.27	2.58	2.31	
6	1.81	1.84	1.78	
4	1.41	1.46	1.48	
2	1.09	1.18	1.12	
0	0.70	0.68	0.72	

a Circle the value in the table which is anomalous.

b Suggest a reason for the anomalous value.

c Calculate the mean drop time for each wing length, ignoring the anomalous value. Write your answers in the table.

d Write a conclusion from the results in the table.

e Discuss your conclusion with a partner to see how you could improve it. Mark any corrections to your conclusion clearly.

f Explain the importance of your conclusion for seed dispersal.

5 Describe *two* ways, other than spinners, in which plants disperse their seeds.

6a What protects tomato seeds?

b Why do the seeds need protection?

1 The table shows a 'confidence grid'. Tick (✓) *one* box for each statement in the table.

Statement	Definitely correct	Might be correct	Might be wrong	Definitely wrong
a During germination, enzymes break down food stores in a seed to produce glucose.				
b Mitochondria in plant embryo cells carry out photosynthesis.				
c Dormant seeds are not alive because they are not growing.				
d Seeds need mineral salts from the soil to make proteins and oils in order to germinate.				

2a Seeds carry out respiration. Complete the word equation for respiration:

glucose + oxygen → _____

b Explain why seeds carry out respiration.

_____

_____

3a Complete this word equation for photosynthesis.

_____ + water → _____ + glucose

b Describe the function of chlorophyll in photosynthesis.

_____

4a What additional resources does a seedling need compared with a germinating seed?

_____

b Why does it need these extra resources?

_____

_____

SB

1 What is the point of giving organisms scientific names?

2a Explain why conifers and mosses are classified in the same kingdom.

b Describe *one* feature that you can use to identify a plant as a conifer.

3 The diagram outlines the life cycle of a flowering plant.

Label the diagram clearly to show when the following happen: pollination, fertilisation, seed dispersal, germination.

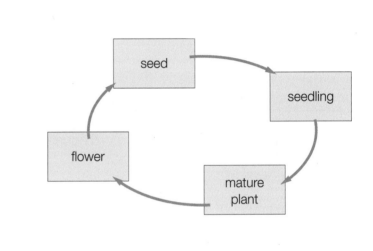

4a Explain how plants make glucose.

b Explain why plants need to make glucose.

5a Describe *two* ways that animals use plants other than for food.

b Use your answer to part **a** to help explain why plant biodiversity is important.

1a Here is the start of a concept map on respiration. Work with a partner to add suitable words from what you have learned before, including breathing and gas exchange. Add comments to explain the links between the words.

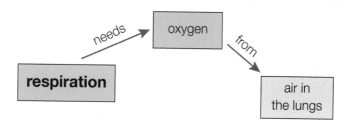

b Compare your concept map with other students and add anything else that you think is useful.

2a When someone starts to do exercise, what happens to their breathing and heartbeat rates?

b Explain why these rates change.

8Ca AEROBIC RESPIRATION

SB **1** Beaker X contains peas that are starting to grow. Beaker Y contains boiled peas. In which beaker will:

a the temperature rise? Explain your reasoning.

....

....

....

b carbon dioxide be made? Explain your reasoning.

....

....

....

2 Use words from the box to complete the text. Words may be used more than once.

ATP	carbon dioxide	glucose	energy	oxygen	water

Aerobic respiration is a series of reactions in cells that requires a gas called

.... This gas is used to break down ....

into .... and .... The process releases

...., which is transferred to molecules of ....

These molecules carry the .... around the cell to wherever it is needed for

making other cell processes happen.

SB **3a** Write out the word equation for aerobic respiration.

....

b Suggest *one* way in which this is a good model for respiration and *one* way in which it is a poor one.

....

....

....

8Cb GAS EXCHANGE SYSTEM

1 Draw *one* line from each word to its definition.

Scientific term	Definition
ventilation	breathing out
respiration	movements of the diaphragm and ribcage
breathing	air movement into and out of the lungs
exhalation	breakdown of glucose in cells to release energy

2 The diagrams show how breathing causes ventilation of the lungs.

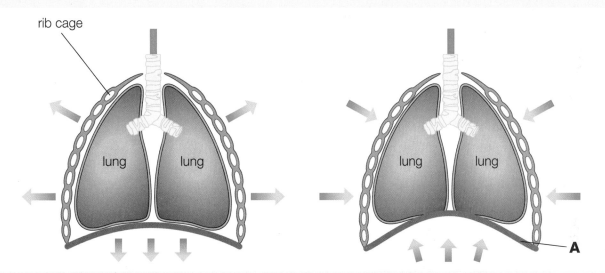

a Name the part labelled A. _____

b Add an arrow head to the blue line above each trachea to show the direction of movement of air into or out of the lungs.

c Discuss with a partner how the air pressure inside your lungs is changed and how this causes air to move. Agree a description of what happens when you breathe in and write it here.

_____

_____

d Describe the function of the cartilage around the trachea.

_____

3 How are cells in the gas exchange system specialised to keep the lungs clean?

_____

8Cb GAS EXCHANGE IN THE LUNGS

SB

1 Complete the sentences using words from the box.

alveoli	blood	carbon dioxide	diffusion	oxygen	random

Gas exchange in the lungs occurs by a process called ...., which

happens because of the continuous .... movement of molecules.

There are more .... molecules in the blood than in the air in the

.... so more molecules move into the air from the blood than in the opposite

direction. There are more .... molecules in the air than in the blood, so there

is overall movement of those molecules into the ....

2 Explain how having many alveoli is an adaptation of the lungs for gas exchange.

....

....

3 The diagram shows an air sac in the lungs and an alveolus.

a Name the gases on the diagram.

X ....

Y ....

b Explain the importance of each air sac being surrounded by a network of capillaries.

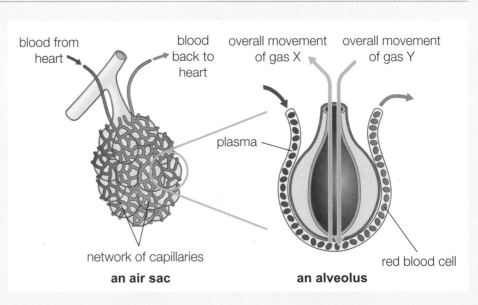

blood from heart

blood back to heart

overall movement of gas X

overall movement of gas Y

plasma

network of capillaries

red blood cell

an air sac

an alveolus

c Explain how the walls of a capillary and an alveolus are adapted for gas exchange.

....

....

SB

4 Explain why gas exchange can be reduced in smokers.

....

....

8Cb MEANS AND RANGES (WS)

1 Tick (✓) the term that means the amount of air that is breathed in and out with each breath.

- ☐ **A** breathing rate
- ☐ **B** tidal volume
- ☐ **C** total lung volume
- ☐ **D** ventilation depth

2 Hitesh and Josie measured their tidal volumes just before and just after exercise. Their results are shown in the table.

	Tidal volume (cm³)				
	1st try	**2nd try**	**3rd try**	**4th try**	**mean**
Hitesh before exercise	450	440	420	430	
Josie before exercise	350	350	310	300	
Hitesh after exercise	1010	1100	1050	990	
Josie after exercise	750	950	840	900	

a Calculate the range of each set of results.

Hitesh just before _____ Hitesh just after _____

Josie just before _____ Josie just after _____

b Which set of results can you be most sure of being correct. Explain your reasoning.

_____

_____

c Complete the table by calculating the mean value for each set of results.

d Explain why it is useful to use the mean value when discussing these results.

_____

_____

e Use the mean values in the table to write a conclusion.

_____

_____

f Compare your conclusion to others in your group. If you can, write down *one* way in which you could improve your conclusion.

_____

1 The table shows how a student's pulse rate changed over 50 minutes, during which time she did some running.

Time (minutes)	0	5	10	15	20	25	30	35	40	45	50
pulse rate (beats per min)	62	63	62	86	112	115	114	95	84	69	62

a With a partner, discuss a method for this investigation that would give repeatable results. Write your method below.

....

....

b Calculate the student's mean resting pulse rate from the data in the table. Show your working.

....

c Draw a line graph of the results on the grid.

d Use your graph to identify when exercise started and ended.

start .... end ....

e Explain why the pulse rate changes with exercise as shown in the graph.

....

....

1 Correct the mistake in each of these sentences.

a Oxygen is carried by haemoglobin in white blood cells.

b Blood that is carrying a lot of oxygen is dark red.

c Carbon dioxide is a reactant in aerobic respiration.

d Substances are exchanged between tissues and blood in veins.

2a Write *one* other sentence about blood vessels that contains a mistake.

....

b Ask a partner to spot the mistake, then to mark the correction to your sentence.

3 Number the statements in order to show how blood in the lungs circulates through the body back to the lungs. The first one has been done for you.

| 1 | Blood is carried from the lungs in blood vessels to the heart.

☐ The heart pumps the blood to the lungs.

☐ Capillaries connect to form veins, which carry blood back to the heart.

☐ The heart pumps the blood through arteries to other parts of the body.

☐ Blood flows through the tissues in capillaries.

4 Explain why the amount of carbon dioxide in your blood increases when you run upstairs.

....

....

5 Explain why a boy's breathing rate doubles during a swimming race.

....

....

....

1 Explain why an asthma attack causes shortness of breath. To answer this, tick (✓) *one* box for each of parts **a** and **b** below.

a In an asthma attack:
- ☐ **A** the breathing tubes get wider.
- ☐ **B** the breathing tubes get narrower.
- ☐ **C** the diaphragm stops working.
- ☐ **D** the lungs shrink.

b This means that:
- ☐ **A** too much air gets into the lungs.
- ☐ **B** much less air gets into the lungs.
- ☐ **C** the pulse rate decreases.
- ☐ **D** the lungs stop breathing in oxygen.

SB

2a Why does blood from a smoker contain less oxygen than blood from a non-smoker? Give as many reasons as you can.

....

....

b Discuss your reasons with a partner to see if they have anything different. If possible, write *one* more reason that you did not have in part **a**.

....

3a Explain why smokers are more likely than non-smokers to develop cardiovascular disease.

....

....

b Explain why cardiovascular disease can cause cells to die.

....

....

4 Complete the sentences using words from the box.

| faster | increases | larger | less | more | slower | reduces |

Emphysema is damage to the lungs that .... the surface area for gas

exchange. So oxygen diffusion into the body is .... than normal. This means

.... oxygen gets into the body with each breath, so the person has to

breathe .... to get enough oxygen into their blood.

1 Give the meaning of vital capacity.

2a Carry out the practical to collect measurements of vital capacity for as many people as you can. Construct a spreadsheet like the one below. Add columns for other measurements that you think might affect vital capacity.

	A	B	C	D	E
	name	vital capacity	age	height	
1					
2					

b Write suitable units in the table beside the variables.

c Collect measurements from as many different people as you can. Add their measurements to your spreadsheet. Then construct scatter graphs from your spreadsheet and look for any correlations.

Describe *one* correlation you have found.

3 The scatter graph shows the results from a study on vital capacity in a large group of young men.

a Draw a line of best fit on the scatter graph.

b Describe the relationship shown in the scatter graph.

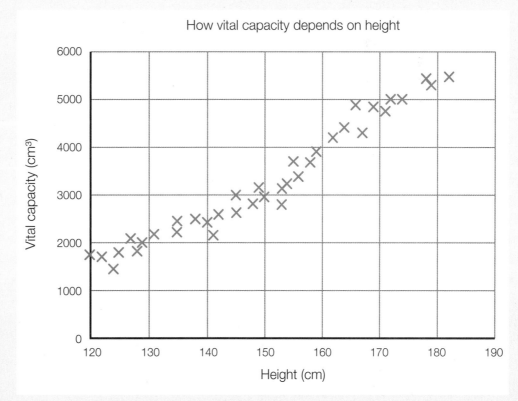

How vital capacity depends on height

c Compare *your* results with the scatter graph above. Comment on any similarities or differences.

1 This apparatus is used to compare air that is breathed in and breathed out.

a Name an indicator that could be used to replace limewater to test for the presence of carbon dioxide.

b A student breathes gently through the apparatus for 2 minutes. Describe any changes to the limewater that would be seen in each tube. Explain your answer.

mouthpiece

limewater

boiling tube A   boiling tube B

2 Explain why the temperature of exhaled air is usually warmer than that of inhaled air.

3 Plant leaves have many stomata in their lower surface for gas exchange.

a Describe how gases enter and leave the leaf.

b Tick (✓) *one* box to show when respiration happens in plant cells.

☐ **A** only at night   ☐ **B** only in daylight   ☐ **C** all the time   ☐ **D** never

c A plant is placed in a sealed container with a beaker of yellow hydrogen carbonate indicator. At sunset the following day the indicator is pink. Explain this observation.

8Ce ANAEROBIC RESPIRATION

1 Discuss with a partner what happens in aerobic respiration and anaerobic respiration. Then tick (✓) the correct box in each row.

	Only aerobic	Only anaerobic	Both aerobic and anaerobic
a breaks down glucose	☐	☐	☐
b produces carbon dioxide	☐	☐	☐
c produces lactic acid	☐	☐	☐
d requires oxygen	☐	☐	☐
e releases energy	☐	☐	☐
f occurs in plants and animals	☐	☐	☐

2a State the function of the ATP produced in respiration.

....

b Compare the amount of ATP produced in aerobic and anaerobic respiration.

....

....

3a Suggest why anaerobic respiration is important for a sprint swimmer.

....

....

b Why can't a swimmer sprint for a long time?

....

....

4 What causes EPOC? Give as many reasons as you can.

....

....

....

....

1 Look back at the concept map that you drew in topic **8Ca**.

a Check for any mistakes and make any corrections in a different colour.

b On the lines below, write any new words or ideas that you have learned in this unit. Then see if you can add some of these to your concept map.

....

....

....

....

2 Discuss reasons for the following with a partner. Then write your answers.

a Athletes may do warming-up exercises to raise heart rate and breathing rate before a race.

....

....

b Sprint athletes may not take a breath during their race but their muscles still contract strongly.

....

....

c The average resting heart rate for a young man is 60 beats per minute. The resting heart rate of an athlete may be only 40 beats per minute.

....

....

3 An athlete falls during a race and cuts her leg. Dark red blood flows gently out of the cut. Which type of blood vessel has been damaged? Give a reason for your answer.

....

....

SB **4** Where are the breathing muscles found?

....

....

1 Use the initials to name the seven processes carried out by living things.

M .... R .... S ....

G .... R .... E ....

N ....

2 Draw *one* line from each kingdom to its description.

Kingdom

animals

plants

fungi

protoctists

prokaryotes

Description

mostly single-celled, with nucleus in cell

make own food

feed on living organisms

single-celled, no nucleus in cell

live on dead organisms

3 The diagram shows a human cheek cell. Work with a partner to answer the questions about the cell.

a Describe the function of the:

i cell membrane ....

....

cell membrane

nucleus

cytoplasm containing mitochondria

ii mitochondria. ....

b Name *one* characteristic of a plant cell that is *not* found in an animal cell and describe its function.

....

4a Suggest what the word *microorganism* means.

....

b Describe *one* way in which microorganisms are useful.

....

c Describe *one* way in which microorganisms are harmful.

....

1a Name *one* kingdom that contains only unicellular organisms.

....

b Name *two* structures present in the cells of all kingdoms except prokaryotes.

....

c Cells of plants, fungi and prokaryotes all have cell walls. Explain why they are not all grouped in one kingdom.

....

....

SB

2a Why is there no virus kingdom?

....

b Number the following in order of size, starting with 1 for the largest.

☐ prokaryote cell   ☐ virus   ☐ protoctist cell

3 Label the diagram of a virus.

4a Complete the sentences to explain how a virus makes new viruses.

The virus gets inside a ....

The strand of virus genes causes ....

The new viruses then .... so they can infect other cells.

b Name *one* example of a human disease caused by viruses. ....

c Explain why viruses cause harm to cells.

....

5 Discuss these statements with a partner and then write down what they mean.

a Viruses carry out replication not reproduction.

_____

_____

b Viruses are obligate parasites.

_____

_____

6 Use words from the box to complete the text about diffusion.

| fewer | more | moving | overall |

Diffusion happens because particles are constantly _____. When there are

more particles in one region than another, there will be an overall movement of particles from where there

are _____ to where there are _____.

7 The diagram shows two cubes of clear jelly.

a Which cube has:

i the larger surface area _____

ii the larger volume? _____

b Explain why surface area : volume ratio decreases
as the size of a cube increases.

_____

c The cubes were placed in a beaker of water coloured with a dye. After 30 minutes the dye had reached
the centre of cube A. Colour in cubes A and B to show how far the dye had spread into the cubes in 30
minutes.

d Explain what you have drawn for cube B.

_____

8a Which organ system carries materials to human tissues? _____

b Explain why a unicellular organism does not need a transport system but humans do.

_____

8Da TACKLING DISEASES (STEM)

1 Discuss the following questions with a partner before writing your answers.

a How are vaccines and antibiotics used differently against bacterial diseases?

_____

_____

_____

b How do soaps and disinfectants differ in the way they protect against microorganisms?

_____

_____

_____

SB

2 Why will an antibiotic not cure measles?

_____

SB

3 In a community, a disease is less likely to spread from an infected person if many people have been vaccinated against that disease. Explain this observation.

_____

_____

_____

SB

4 In your experiment on hand washing:

a Which of your methods would be best for removing bacteria from skin?

_____

b Explain how you made this conclusion.

_____

_____

c Which variables did you control to make this a fair test?

_____

_____

8Db MICROSCOPIC FUNGI

1 Complete the word equations for respiration in a yeast cell.

a aerobic respiration:

glucose + ...

b anaerobic respiration (fermentation):

glucose → ....

c Discuss with a partner which type of respiration produces the most ATP. Then write an answer that explains your choice.

....

....

....

2 Name a fungus and the disease that it causes in humans.

....

3 Explain why a new yeast cell formed in asexual reproduction has identical characteristics to the parent cell.

....

....

....

4 Use the letters on the graph to answer the questions.

Circle the correct answers.

a At which point is the yeast population growing fastest?

A   **B**   **C**

b At which point is there no growth in the yeast population?

A   **B**   **C**

c Which resource is most likely to be the limiting factor for the growth of a population of yeast cells?

oxygen   **carbon dioxide**   **glucose**   **ethanol**

How a yeast population changes with time

Number of yeast cells (vertical axis), Time (horizontal axis). Points A, B, C marked on the curve.

1 Use the diagram of a bacterium to answer the questions.

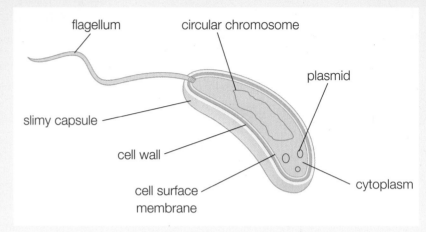

a Which structure is found in the nucleoid region?

b Which structure controls what enters and leaves the cell?

c Which structures protect the bacterium?

d Which structures contain genes?

e What evidence in the diagram shows that this bacterium species can move?

2a Work with a partner to complete the Venn diagram for the parts of plant, animal and bacterial cells. Place shared parts in the overlapping areas.

b Use your diagram to construct a statement key to identify which type of organism a cell comes from. Ask your partner to check your key to make sure it works well.

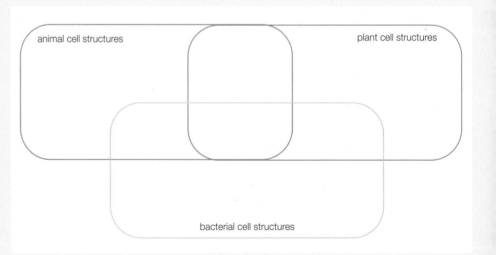

3 Some species of *Lactobacillus* bacteria are used to make yoghurt from milk.

a Circle the product the bacteria make that causes the milk to become sour.

carbon dioxide   **lactic acid**   **ethanol**   **oxygen**

b Name the two-word process that makes this product.

....

c Name *one* other place (in a different organism) where this process happens.

....

4a Use the axes to sketch a graph to show how the numbers of bacterial cells in a jug of fresh milk might change with time.

b Draw a second line to show how the number of bacterial cells in the jug would change in a fridge. Label the lines on the graph clearly.

c Compare your graph with others in your class. Write notes on the graph of any corrections that are needed.

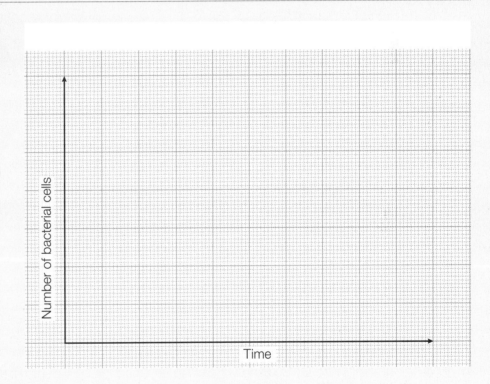

5 Whooping cough is a disease caused by the bacterium *Bordetella pertussis*.

a Describe how you can be protected from becoming ill with whooping cough.

....

b Describe how someone who already has whooping cough could be treated to help kill the bacteria inside them.

....

c Explain why *Bordetella pertussis* is an example of a pathogen.

....

1 Tick (✓) *one* box to show data that would be best presented as a pie chart.
- ☐ **A** The time taken to make yoghurt from milk depending on temperature.
- ☐ **B** The number of deaths from flu infections in each month of the year.
- ☐ **C** The proportions of human infections caused by different bacteria.
- ☐ **D** The number of bacteria in different samples of water.

2 The pie charts show the top 10 causes of death in two different groups of countries in 2016.

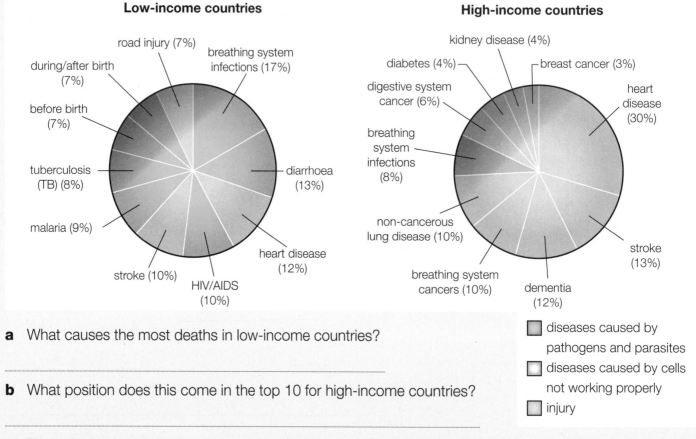

Low-income countries

road injury (7%)
during/after birth (7%)
before birth (7%)
tuberculosis (TB) (8%)
malaria (9%)
stroke (10%)
HIV/AIDS (10%)
heart disease (12%)
diarrhoea (13%)
breathing system infections (17%)

High-income countries

kidney disease (4%)
diabetes (4%)
digestive system cancer (6%)
breathing system infections (8%)
non-cancerous lung disease (10%)
breathing system cancers (10%)
dementia (12%)
stroke (13%)
heart disease (30%)
breast cancer (3%)

a What causes the most deaths in low-income countries?

_____

b What position does this come in the top 10 for high-income countries?

_____

☐ diseases caused by pathogens and parasites
☐ diseases caused by cells not working properly
☐ injury

c The colours show how the diseases can be grouped into different types.

i In low-income countries, calculate the proportion of deaths caused by infectious diseases.

_____

ii Calculate this proportion for high-income countries.

_____

iii How do your answers to parts **i** and **ii** compare?

_____

iv Suggest *one* reason for the differences in the main causes of death in the high- and low-income countries.

_____

8Dd PROTOCTISTS

1 The diagram shows two protoctists found in pond water.

a Why are these two organisms grouped as protoctists?

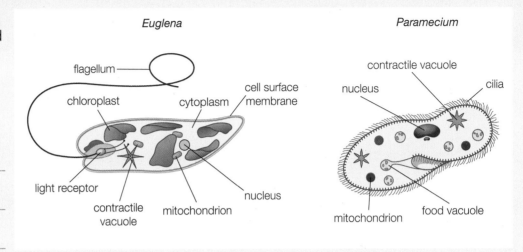

Euglena

flagellum

chloroplast

cytoplasm

cell surface membrane

light receptor

contractile vacuole

mitochondrion

nucleus

Paramecium

contractile vacuole

nucleus

cilia

mitochondrion

food vacuole

....

....

b Which protoctist is the unicellular alga? Give a reason for your answer.

....

....

c Can these protoctists move? Explain your answer.

....

....

2 *Plasmodium* is a protoctist that causes malaria in humans. Discuss these questions with a partner before answering. Use the diagram to help you.

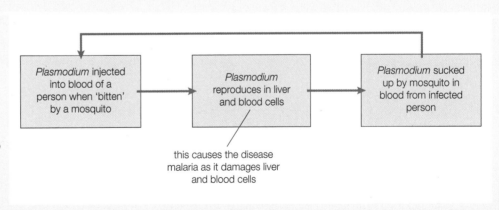

Plasmodium injected into blood of a person when 'bitten' by a mosquito

Plasmodium reproduces in liver and blood cells

Plasmodium sucked up by mosquito in blood from infected person

this causes the disease malaria as it damages liver and blood cells

a Is *Plasmodium* a pathogen? Give a reason for your answer.

....

....

b Is *Plasmodium* an obligate parasite? Give a reason for your answer.

....

....

1a Write a word equation to describe photosynthesis.

....

b Explain the function of chlorophyll in photosynthesis.

....

2 The table shows the biomass of different trophic levels on a coral reef.

Trophic level	producers	primary consumers	secondary consumers
Biomass (g/m²)	703	132	11

a Use the information in the table to draw a pyramid of biomass on the grid.

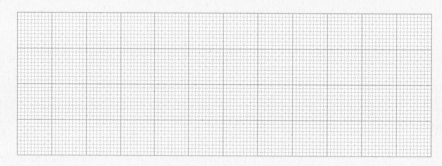

b Explain the shape of the pyramid of biomass.

....

c Most producers on a coral reef are unicellular algae. Explain why pollution that kills the algae is a problem for the reef community.

....

3 Mercury is a poisonous metal that is absorbed from water by algae and stored in their cells. The diagram shows part of an ocean food web. Would a tuna or a salmon contain more mercury? Explain your answer.

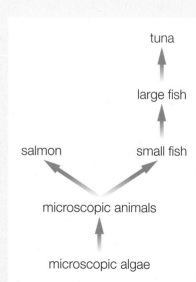

....

....

....

8De DECOMPOSERS AND CARBON

1 Tick (✓) *one* box to show the definition of decomposer.
  ☐ **A** something that breaks down easily in the environment
  ☐ **B** an organism that breaks down the tissues of dead organisms
  ☐ **C** an animal that eats dead animals
  ☐ **D** a plant that captures animals to eat

2 Some of these statements about the carbon cycle contain mistakes. Discuss the sentences with a partner and mark any corrections.

a The process that takes carbon dioxide from the air is respiration.

b The only organisms that take carbon dioxide from the air are producers.

c Fossil fuels contain very little carbon.

d The only process that adds carbon dioxide to the air is combustion.

e When decomposers cause decay, they release carbon dioxide through respiration.

3 A gardener builds a compost heap using kitchen and garden waste.
a Explain why covering the heap with a blanket causes compost to form faster.

....

....

b Explain why the gardener will spread the compost over the soil where plants are growing.

....

....

4 Name the type of molecule that a fungus uses to break down large organic molecules into smaller ones.

....

5 In the last 300 years, the amount of carbon dioxide in the atmosphere has increased. Suggest why.

....

....

1a Write down the most important point you learned about each of the following.

Topic	Important point
viruses	
diffusion	
microscopic fungi (e.g. yeast)	
fermentation	
growth curves	
bacteria	
protoctists	
pyramid of biomass	
decomposers	
carbon cycle	

b Compare your points with other students to check they are correct. Mark any corrections in a different colour.

SB

2 Scientists find many different types of microorganisms underground. However, they do not find living algae. Explain why.

1 Use a *pencil* to tick (✓) *one* answer to each of the following questions.

a Combustion is best described as:
- ☐ **A** a physical change.
- ☐ **B** decay.
- ☐ **C** a chemical reaction.
- ☐ **D** a change of state.

b A gas in the air that is required for combustion is:
- ☐ **A** nitrogen.
- ☐ **B** oxygen.
- ☐ **C** carbon dioxide.
- ☐ **D** methane.

c Magnesium oxide is:
- ☐ **A** an element.
- ☐ **B** a mixture.
- ☐ **C** a non-metal.
- ☐ **D** a compound.

d Hydrogen powered vehicles may become more popular that petrol or diesel ones because:
- ☐ **A** hydrogen is an explosive gas.
- ☐ **B** hydrogen does not cause pollution when it burns.
- ☐ **C** hydrogen is cheaper than petrol.
- ☐ **D** hydrogen is lighter than air.

2 Ask your teacher how many of your answers to question **1** are correct. Then work with others and the Student Book to identify your incorrect answers. Make corrections and check with your teacher. Do this until they are all correct.

3 Why are the fuels used in most modern cars harmful to the environment?

....
....
....
....

4 Write the word equation for when hydrogen burns in air.

....

5 A student burns a fuel and collects the gases that are produced. She thinks that one gas might be carbon dioxide. Explain how she could test for this gas.

....
....

6 Explain how the fuel in a car is used to make it move.

....
....

8Ea BURNING FUELS

SB **1** Define the word *fuel*.

SB **2** What is the product of the reaction in a hydrogen fuel cell?

3 Explain how products are formed when a hydrocarbon fuel combusts. To answer this, tick (✔) *one* box for each of parts **a** and **b** below:

a The products are:
- ☐ **A** hydrogen and carbon dioxide.
- ☐ **B** carbon and hydroxide.
- ☐ **C** carbon dioxide and water.
- ☐ **D** hydrogen and carbon.

b This is because:
- ☐ **A** oxygen is removed.
- ☐ **B** carbon dioxide reacts with the hydrogen atoms.
- ☐ **C** oxygen reacts with the carbon atoms and hydrogen atoms.
- ☐ **D** hydrogen reacts with the carbon atoms and oxygen atoms.

4 Write down a reason why hydrogen might be dangerous to use as a fuel in cars.

5 Describe the tests for the following gases and their positive results.

a hydrogen:

b carbon dioxide:

6 Fuels A, B and C were burnt and the products were added to blue cobalt chloride. The table shows the results.

One fuel is a hydrocarbon. Explain which fuel is the hydrocarbon.

Fuel	Colour of cobalt chloride at end
A	blue
B	blue
C	pink

7 When blue copper sulfate is heated, it turns white and releases water vapour which condenses back to liquid water when it is cooled.

a What name is given to the water that is lost from the blue copper sulfate?

b What happens if you add the water back to the white powder?

1 What element is added to aluminium when it takes part in an oxidation reaction? _____

2 One carbon atom reacts with one oxygen molecule to produce one molecule of the product. Draw a diagram to show this reaction. (*Hint*: A carbon atom is shown as a single circle.)

3 Write word equations for the reaction of each of these metals with oxygen:

a magnesium _____

b iron _____

c copper _____

4 What does the *law of conservation of mass* tell us? _____

_____

5 Complete the table.

Reaction	Mass of metal	Mass of oxygen	Mass of oxide
magnesium + oxygen	24 g	16 g	
iron + oxygen	56 g		72 g
copper + oxygen		32 g	96 g

6 Many years ago, an opponent of the phlogiston theory wrote an explanation of why the phlogiston theory is wrong. Complete the gaps using words from the box.

burns	heavier	increases	oxygen	phlogiston

The phlogiston theory says that _____ escapes when something

_____ . But magnesium gets _____ as it burns.

Supporters of the theory say that in this case the phlogiston has a negative mass! A much better

explanation is that magnesium gains _____ from the air so that its mass

_____ .

7 Magnesium reacts vigorously with oxygen, releasing a lot of energy. Describe *one* way in which energy is transferred when magnesium oxidises.

_____

1a Use a *pencil* to tick (✓) the boxes to show if these statements are true or false.

Statement		True	False
i	iron + oxygen → iron oxate	☐	☐
ii	In an oxidation reaction, oxygen is added to one of the reactants.	☐	☐
iii	During an oxidation reaction, metal atoms grow in size.	☐	☐
iv	The products in an oxidation reaction are always heavier than the reactants.	☐	☐
v	Non-metals, such as hydrogen, also form oxides.	☐	☐
vi	56 g of zinc reacts with 16 g of oxygen to make 82 g of zinc oxide.	☐	☐

b Ask your teacher how many of your answers are correct. Then work with others and the Student Book to identify your incorrect answers. Make corrections and check with your teacher. Do this until they are all correct.

c Choose one of the incorrect statements and write a correct version. Discuss your answer with others in your group to check.

2 A scientist conducts some experiments with a mystery element X. The table shows the results when the scientist heats 'X' in air.

Mass of X (g)	Mass of product (g)
40	56
30	42
20	28
10	14

a Describe the pattern of the results. _____

b Suggest what happens to the mystery element when it is heated. _____

c What mass of oxygen would combine with 120 g of X?

3 The diagram shows the reaction between hydrogen and oxygen. State the number of:

a different elements in water _____

b oxygen molecules to oxidise two hydrogen molecules

_____

c hydrogen atoms in a water molecule _____

d atoms in an oxygen molecule. _____

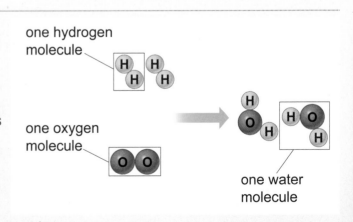

one hydrogen molecule

one oxygen molecule

one water molecule

8Ec FIRE SAFETY

1 Combustion is an exothermic reaction. What does exothermic mean?

....

2a Complete this fire triangle diagram.

b Explain how to use the fire triangle to remember how to put out a fire.

....

....

....

....

FUEL

3 Explain one way of putting out a *large* fire of wood and paper.
To answer this, tick (✓) *one* box for each of parts **a** and **b** below.

a A way to put out this fire is to:
- ☐ **A** cover it with a blanket.
- ☐ **B** put water on it.
- ☐ **C** put petrol on it.
- ☐ **D** use a fan to blow on it.

b This works because:
- ☐ **A** oxygen is added.
- ☐ **B** oxygen and heat are removed.
- ☐ **C** fuel is removed.
- ☐ **D** fire is removed.

4 Write down the meaning of each of these hazard symbols in the spaces below.

	a	b	c
Symbol			
Name			

5a Explain why an oil fire should *not* be treated with a water-filled fire extinguisher.

....

....

....

....

b Tick (✓) *one* box to show your level of confidence about fire and fire safety.

- ☐ I am confident of teaching the class about this idea.
- ☐ I am confident about contributing to a group discussion about this idea.
- ☐ I would rather work with someone else on this idea.

SB

1 In the experiment shown in the diagram, two variables are the volume of fuel burnt and the time it takes for all the fuel to burn.

a Which of these is the independent variable and which is the dependent variable?

i independent variable: ....

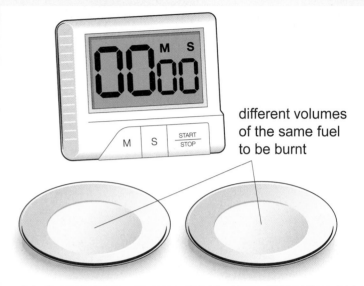

different volumes of the same fuel to be burnt

ii dependent variable: ....

b One variable that should be controlled is the type of fuel. Explain how using different fuels might affect the dependent variable.

....

....

c Describe *one* other variable that should be controlled in this experiment and what effect it might have if it were not controlled properly.

....

....

....

2 The table shows a 'confidence grid'. Tick (✓) *one* box for each statement.

Statement	Is definitely correct	Might be correct	Might be wrong	Is definitely wrong
a The independent variable does not change because of anything the experimenter does.				
b The dependent variable is the variable the experimenter measures.				
c The dependent variable is changed when the independent variable changes.				
d A control variable is fixed so that it can change the dependent variable in the correct way.				

3 Use words from the box to complete the sentences. You can use the words more than once.

| control | dependent | fair | independent | valid |

In an experiment you need to stop the _____ variables changing. This is so that

only the _____ variable causes changes in the _____

variable. A test like this is a _____ test and is one that produces the data that it

is supposed to. A _____ test produces _____ data.

4 Some students recorded the time 10 g of different fuels burnt and the highest temperature reached by a beaker of water heated by each fuel. They wrote:

Fuel C burnt for six minutes and fuel D burnt for half as long, and fuel D only heated the water to 26 °C but fuel C heated it to 71 °C. 10 g of fuel A burnt for 7 minutes and the water reached 63 °C. Fuel B heated the water to 55 °C and burnt for 4 and half minutes.

Design a table to present these results. Use the grid below.

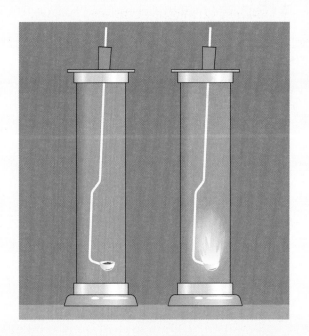

5 Some students wanted to find out if different metals burnt for different lengths of time in oxygen. They lowered samples of hot metals into gas jars of oxygen (shown in the diagram). They recorded the length of time that each metal burnt. Write down *three* control variables for this investigation, and how to control each.

Control variable	How it is controlled

8Ed AIR POLLUTION

SB 1 Name the carbon-containing compounds produced by an engine in which there is incomplete combustion of a hydrocarbon fuel.

2 Complete this table. Write the name of each molecule in the space provided.

	a C O	**b** O C O	**c** O O	**d** O S O
Name				

SB **3a** Suggest an example of a nitrogen oxide and draw a diagram of it in the box.

b Explain why vehicle engines produce nitrogen oxides.

c Write down *one* way in which harmful emissions from car engines are reduced.

4 Tick (✓) the *best* description of a catalyst. A catalyst:
- ☐ **A** reacts with substances that cause air pollution.
- ☐ **B** slows down reactions that produce pollutants.
- ☐ **C** is a type of filter found on vehicle exhausts.
- ☐ **D** speeds up a reaction but is not used up or changed.

5 Explain how acid rain is formed. To answer this, tick (✓) *one* box for each of parts **a** and **b** below.

a Certain gases dissolve in water vapour in the air including:
- ☐ **A** carbon monoxide.
- ☐ **B** sulfur dioxide.
- ☐ **C** soot.
- ☐ **D** hydrogen.

b This causes rain that:
- ☐ **A** has a pH of about 7.
- ☐ **B** has a higher pH than usual.
- ☐ **C** has a lower pH than usual.
- ☐ **D** needs to be neutralised with an acid.

6 Acidic waste gases from a power station chimney can be neutralised by sprays of calcium hydroxide before they are released into the atmosphere. Complete the word equation to show this reaction:

nitric acid + calcium hydroxide →

7 Tick (✓) the breathing problem caused by air pollution.

- ☐ **A** asthma
- ☐ **B** bronchitis
- ☐ **C** cancer
- ☐ **D** diabetes

8 Look at the graph.

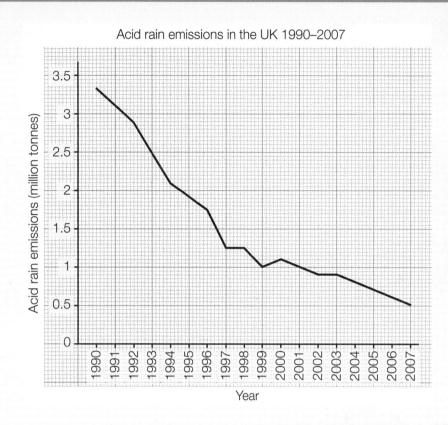

Acid rain emissions in the UK 1990–2007

a Complete the gaps in the sentences below using words and figures from the box. You may use them once, more than once or not at all.

0.5	3.3	10	15	17	50	85	2002	2007	emissions	decreased

million   increased   tonnes

The line graph gives information about acid rain _____ over a

_____ year period in the UK. The total amount of acid rain emissions

_____ nearly every year between 1990 and _____ .

In 1990, the total of acid rain emissions was _____ tonnes. This figure fell to

_____ million _____ in 2007. This is a reduction of

_____ %.

b Suggest *one* reason for this change in emissions.

_____

SB **1** Where does most of the energy that warms the Earth's surface come from?

SB **2a** Explain how carbon dioxide in the air helps to cause the greenhouse effect.

b Share your answers to part **a** with others. Discuss which answers are best and why, then write down *one* way in which you could improve your original answer.

3 Look at this graph and answer the questions below.

a What does this graph tell us about the concentration of carbon dioxide in the atmosphere?

b Why does the shape of this graph concern scientists?

4 Suggest *two* effects of global warming in countries near where you live.

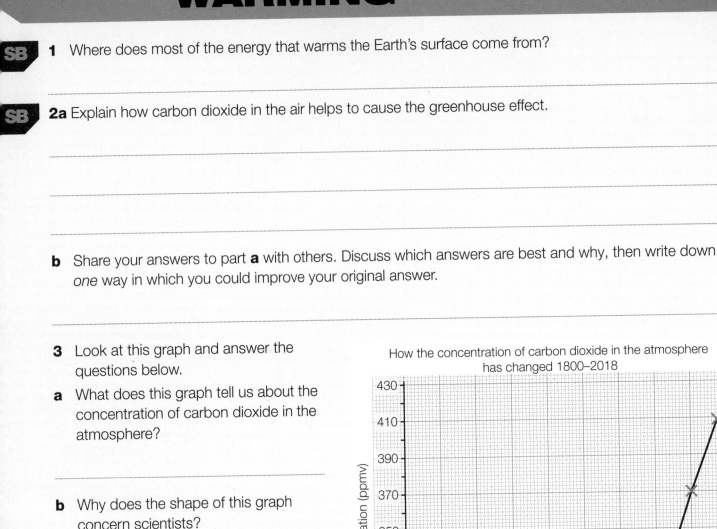

How the concentration of carbon dioxide in the atmosphere has changed 1800–2018

5 Calcium carbonate (limestone) is heated during the production of cement. It undergoes thermal decomposition. Explain why cement production contributes to global warming.

1 What is the *carbon footprint* of a business or organisation?

2 Explain why some companies encourage their employees to use car sharing schemes. This is when two or more employees travel to and from work in the same car, rather than each taking their own cars.

3a Suggest why eating locally-grown food reduces your carbon footprint.

b Find out how far some of your food has travelled (its food miles) and write your data in the table.

c Use your data to state and explain *one* way to reduce your carbon footprint.

Food	Distance travelled to your plate

4 You are going to work in a group to prepare a poster or presentation slide for your school's management team on how to reduce your school's carbon footprint. Explain *four* important points that you want to include on your poster.

SB

1 Some new cars have stop–start technology, where the engine stops when the car is not moving (such as at traffic lights). State the advantages:

a for the driver

....

....

b for the local population.

....

....

2 Substances A–D were heated in air. The products were then tested with limewater, blue cobalt chloride and dilute acid. The table shows the results.

Write the correct letter from the table to identify each of these substances:

carbon ....

calcium carbonate ....

magnesium ....   methane ....

Substance	Results of tests on products		
	added to limewater	added to blue cobalt chloride	reaction with dilute acid
A	turns milky	no change	no reaction
B	no change	no change	reacts
C	turns milky	turns pink	no reaction
D	turns milky	no change	reacts

3 Explain why the products of incomplete combustion are different from those of complete combustion. To answer this, tick (✔) *one* box for each of parts **a** and **b** below.

a The products of incomplete combustion include:
- ☐ **A** methane and carbon monoxide.
- ☐ **B** carbon and hydrogen.
- ☐ **C** carbon and carbon monoxide.
- ☐ **D** carbon dioxide and carbon trioxide.

b This is because:
- ☐ **A** a different fuel is used.
- ☐ **B** there is not enough oxygen.
- ☐ **C** there is too much heat.
- ☐ **D** there is not enough carbon.

4 Most petrol sold around the world has had the sulfur impurities removed from it. What pollutant would be formed by car engines if this was not done?

....

5 Describe *one* way in which a catalyst helps to reduce pollution from a vehicle engine.

....

....

8Fa FIREWORKS

1 Describe the difference between an element and a compound.

_____

_____

_____

2 Tick (✔) the statement that best explains what a chemical reaction is.

☐ **A** when two mixtures are heated together
☐ **B** when the atoms in substances are heated together
☐ **C** when substances are heated to make a new substance
☐ **D** when the atoms rearrange to make new substances

3 Tick (✔) the statement that best explains what a physical change is

☐ **A** a change from an element to a compound
☐ **B** a change from a mixture to a compound
☐ **C** a change from one state to another
☐ **D** a change where no new substances are made

4 Write down _two_ observations you might make that would suggest a chemical change is happening.

_____

_____

5 Ice becomes liquid when it gets warm, and water bubbles when it boils. Are these chemical reactions? Discuss this in your group. Cross out the incorrect answers in the sentences then write your agreed answer below.

Ice becoming liquid _is / is not_ a chemical change.

Water bubbling when it boils _is / is not_ a chemical change.

We think this because: _____

_____

_____

6 In certain fireworks, carbon, sulfur and aluminium react with oxygen.

Write word equations for these three reactions.

_____

_____

1 Complete the following sentences using words from the box. Use each word only once.

atom	element	joined	reactions	substances	two

Each element is made up of just one type of .... All the

atoms in any particular .... are identical. Compounds contain

.... or more elements that are chemically ....

Atoms are not created or destroyed during chemical ....; they are rearranged

to make new ....

SB

2a Draw a table to compare the physical properties of metals and non-metals.

b Share your table with others in your group. Try to add to your table.

3 Find the symbols of the following elements on the periodic table on page 150.

a magnesium ....   **b** sulfur ....   **c** carbon ....   **d** gallium ....

4 6.4 g of copper metal reacts with 1.6 g of oxygen in a sealed container.

a Calculate the mass of copper oxide that you expect to be formed.

b Draw a smile on the face in the box to show how confident you are in your answer – the bigger the smile, the more confident you are.

1 Think about the element magnesium.

a List *two physical* properties of magnesium metal.

....

....

b List *two chemical* properties of magnesium metal.

....

....

2 When 4 g of zinc reacts with 1 g of oxygen, what mass of zinc oxide is produced?

....

3 Complete the table below:

Name			ammonia	methanol
Number of atoms				
Chemical formula				

4 Look at this word equation: carbon + oxygen → carbon dioxide

a Draw a diagram to show how the atoms are rearranged in the reaction. The formula of oxygen is O_2.

b Compare your diagram with others in your group and discuss any differences. Make changes to your diagram if you need to and record what you have changed.

8Fc MENDELEEV'S TABLE

1 Complete the following sentences using words from the box. Use each word only once.

elements	discovered	mass	Mendeleev	periodic	properties

When he published his .... table, Dmitri ....

placed the .... in order of the .... of the atoms.

He grouped elements with similar .... together, and realised that he needed

to leave gaps for elements that were yet to be ....

SB

2 Describe *one* chemical property of:

a the halogens

....

b the alkali metals

....

c the noble gases.

....

3 The noble gases are in the last group of the periodic table, in the furthest right column. Tick (✓) the property which best describes the members of this group:

☐ **A** reactive   ☐ **B** unreactive   ☐ **C** radioactive   ☐ **D** unactive

4 Lithium is in group 1 of the periodic table.

a A teacher placed some lithium in water and a chemical reaction occurred. Write down *one observation* you might make.

....

b Name *one* other metal you would expect to react in a similar way.

....

c Give a reason for your choice of metal in part **b**.

....

5 Complete these word equations.

sodium + water → ....

zinc + chlorine → ....

6 Use a *pencil* to tick (✓) *one* answer to each of the following questions.

a Name an element which is a noble gas.
- ☐ **A** chlorine
- ☐ **B** oxygen
- ☐ **C** radium
- ☐ **D** radon

b Name an element which is an alkali metal.
- ☐ **A** magnesium
- ☐ **B** calcium
- ☐ **C** potassium
- ☐ **D** aluminium

c Give a physical property of the alkali metals.
- ☐ **A** very hard
- ☐ **B** electrical conductors
- ☐ **C** magnetic
- ☐ **D** unreactive

d Give a chemical property of the alkali metals.
- ☐ **A** electrical conductors
- ☐ **B** react with oil
- ☐ **C** react with water
- ☐ **D** soft

e Name an element that was in Mendeleev's original table.
- ☐ **A** bromine
- ☐ **B** xenon
- ☐ **C** gallium
- ☐ **D** scandium

f Chlorine will react with most metals to form a compound with a name ending in:
- ☐ **A** chloride.
- ☐ **B** chlorate.
- ☐ **C** chlorite.
- ☐ **D** chlorine.

7 Ask your teacher how many of your answers to question **6** are correct. Then work with others and the Student Book to identify your incorrect answers. Make corrections and check with your teacher. Do this until they are all correct.

8Fc ANOMALOUS RESULTS (WS)

1 A teacher added lithium metal to water. She collected the gas and measured its volume. The table shows her results:

a Plot a scatter graph of these results. Put mass on the horizontal axis and the dependent variable on the vertical axis.

b Label the anomalous result on your graph.

c Draw a line of best fit; leave out the anomalous result.

Mass of lithium metal (g)	**Volume of gas collected (cm^3)**
0.1	139
0.2	138
0.3	417
0.4	557
0.5	696

d Suggest *one* error that might have caused the anomalous result.

....

....

e Compare your graph with others in your group and discuss any differences. Write down *one* thing that is hard to get right when drawing scatter graphs.

....

1 Look at the graph. It shows what happens when a solid element is heated until it first melts and then boils.

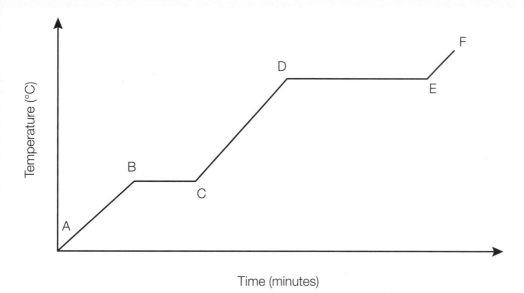

Time (minutes)

a Which line, AB, BC, CD, DE or EF, represents the melting point? ....

b Which line, AB, BC, CD, DE or EF, represents the boiling point? ....

c What state is the substance in between C and D? ....

d Draw a diagram to show how the particles are arranged between A and B.

e At which letter will the particles have the least amount of energy? ....

f Explain why the temperature of the liquid does not change as it boils.

....

....

....

8Fd LOOKING FOR TRENDS

1 Sodium melts at 98 °C and boils at 883 °C.

a What is the freezing point of sodium?

....

b What state will sodium be in at 95 °C?

....

2 Gallium melts at 30 °C and boils at 2400 °C.
What state will gallium be in:

a at room temperature, 25 °C ....

b if held in the palm of someone's hand, assuming skin temperature is about 34 °C?

....

3 The boiling points of some elements in group 7 are: bromine (59 °C), chlorine (−35 °C), fluorine (−188 °C), iodine (184 °C).

a Describe the trend in the boiling point down group 7.

....

b Which element is most likely to be a liquid in the classroom?

....

4 Look at the periodic table on page 150. Write down the name and symbol of the element that is in:

a group 1, period 2 ....

b group 2, period 3 ....

c group 7, period 2 ....

d group 0, period 4. ....

5 Look at the periodic table on page 150. Name and give the symbol for an element that is:

a in the same group as carbon

....

b in the same period as sulfur.

....

1 Yuri Oganessian is a Russian nuclear physicist, who researches super heavy chemical elements. Look at the periodic table on page 150 and find the element that is named after him. Write down its atomic number, name and symbol.

2 Rutherfordium is named after Ernest Rutherford. About a teacher, he said:

"Professor Bickerton's genuine enthusiasm for science gave me a stimulus to start investigations of my own."

Suggest *two* ways in which Prof. Bickerton may have shown his enthusiasm.

3 Work in a group to draw a diagram explaining how new elements are made. Do not use words.

4 Work in a group to show the information in the table as symbols. Use as few words as possible.

	High / low melting points	Strong / ductile / malleable/brittle	Shiny (when polished) / dull	Conductors / insulators
Metals				
Non-metals				

1 There are trends in the properties of the alkali metals in the periodic table.

a Complete the sentence below by crossing out the incorrect word.

As we go down the group, the alkali metals become *more / less reactive*.

SB

b The fourth alkali metal, rubidium, also reacts with water.

i Name the two products formed.

....

ii What would you expect to see during this reaction?

....

c Suggest why the elements in group 1 are called the alkali metals.

....

2 A scientist reacts two elements, a silvery metal and a gas, with oxygen. She then adds water to each of the compounds that have been formed. The compounds dissolve and she tests these solutions with phenolphthalein.

a Fill in the table below using the information given.

Phenolphthalein is pink at pH 8 and above, and colourless below pH 8.

Element that was reacted with oxygen	Colour of solution with phenolphthalein	Acidic or alkaline solution?
silvery metal	pink	
gas	colourless	

b State where, roughly, you would expect to find these elements in the periodic table. Give reasons for your answers.

i The metal would be found .... because

....

ii The gas would be found .... because

....

3 Acids react with different substances.

a Tick (✓) *one* box to answer the following question. When an acid reacts with an alkali the reaction is called:

☐ **A** decomposition.
☐ **B** neutralisation.
☐ **C** indication.
☐ **D** displacement.

b Complete this general word equation.

acid + base → ....

4 When acids react, salts form. The type of salt depends on the reactants.

a Complete the table with the salt that would form in each case.

Acid	Base	Salt that forms
hydrochloric acid	sodium hydroxide	
nitric acid	potassium hydroxide	
sulfuric acid	copper oxide	

b Write a word equation for the reaction between zinc oxide and hydrochloric acid.

....

5 Explain the pH change of water when carbon dioxide is added to make it 'sparkling'. To answer this, tick (✓) *one* box for each of parts **a** and **b** below.

a The pH:
☐ **A** changes from about 7 to about 4.
☐ **B** changes from about 4 to about 7.
☐ **C** changes from about 7 to about 9.
☐ **D** changes from about 9 to about 7.

b This is because:
☐ **A** oxides of metals are alkaline.
☐ **B** oxides of metals are acidic.
☐ **C** oxides of non-metals are alkaline.
☐ **D** oxides of non-metals are acidic.

6 Hot iron wool produces a yellow flame when it reacts with chlorine. However, iron just glows red when it reacts with bromine.

a Suggest what the reaction of hot iron wool with fluorine might look like.

....

b Explain how you made your prediction.

....

8Fe FIREWORK BAN

1 List the names and symbols of five elements found in fireworks.

i name .... symbol ....

ii name .... symbol ....

iii name .... symbol ....

iv name .... symbol ....

v name .... symbol ....

2 The table contains information about the halogens.

a Describe how the arrangement of the particles changes between the melting point and the boiling point.

....

....

....

....

Element	Atomic number	Melting point (°C)	Boiling point (°C)
fluorine	9	−220	−188
chlorine	17	−102	−34
bromine	35	−7	59
iodine	53	114	184

b What is the freezing point of bromine? ....

c What state will fluorine be in at −180 °C? ....

d Describe the trend in the boiling points of the halogens as you go down the group.

....

....

e Chlorine can form an oxide, Cl_2O. If this were added to water, what pH would you expect the solution to be? Tick (✓) *one* box.

☐ **A** 4 ☐ **B** 7 ☐ **C** 10 ☐ **D** 14

f Fluorine exists as molecules of two fluorine atoms. Write the formula of fluorine.

....

g Tick (✓) the statement that best describes the meaning of 'atomic number'.

☐ **A** The number of atoms in a formula.
☐ **B** The number of protons in a single atom.
☐ **C** The number of neutrons in a single atom.
☐ **D** The mass of a single atom.

1 In the list, tick (✓) all the metals.

☐ **A** aluminium   ☐ **D** lead   ☐ **G** slate
☐ **B** carbon   ☐ **E** nickel   ☐ **H** silver
☐ **C** cotton   ☐ **F** oil   ☐ **I** zinc

2a Name *two* properties of iron that make it suitable for building tall structures.

....

....

b Suggest *one* reason why steel has replaced iron in many modern buildings.

....

....

3a Describe what is meant by a composite material.

....

....

b Give *two* physical properties that may make a composite building material better than steel.

....

4 When magnesium is added to sulfuric acid, bubbles appear. In your groups, discuss what is happening. Record your group's thoughts in the first section below. Ignore the other section for now. There is no right or wrong answer.

Ideas from my group:

....

....

What we now think:

....

....

....

....

8Ga METAL PROPERTIES

1 Draw *one* line from each metal property to an item in which that property is useful. Then draw *one* line from each item to match it with the most suitable metal.

Metal property	Item	Suitable metal
good conductor of heat	frying pan	copper
good electrical conductor	mobile phone cable	gold
malleable and ductile	beams to hold up roofs	iron
shiny	garden fencing wire	silver
strong	jewellery	steel

2 What is the difference between a physical and chemical property?

3 Complete the following word equations.

a sodium + oxygen →

b magnesium + fluorine →

c silver + chlorine →

4 Define what is meant by the term *catalyst*.

5 Give a reason why only small amounts of a catalyst are usually used.

6 Describe *one* process that uses a catalyst.

8Gb CORROSION

1 Describe what rusting is.

....

2 A student put some iron wool in an empty test tube full of air, and then put it upside down in a beaker of water. Over time, the iron rusted and removed the oxygen from the air, allowing water to rise up the tube. At the start there was 36 cm³ of air in the tube and at the end there was 28.8 cm³ of air.

a Calculate the volume of oxygen that was lost. Show your working.

b Calculate the percentage of oxygen in air. Show your working.

3 Give *two* reasons why the corrosion of titanium window frames is not a problem.

....

....

4 Complete the table below.

Metal	Symbol equation for metal reacting with oxygen	Ratio of different atoms in the metal compound
titanium (Ti)	Ti + O$_2$ → TiO$_2$	1:2
manganese (Mn)	→ MnO$_2$	
copper (Cu)	2Cu + O$_2$ → 2CuO	

5 Give the ratio of the two different atoms in aluminium oxide (Al$_2$O$_3$).

....

6 The drawings show two iron nails in different places.

a Explain which nail (X or Y) rusts more quickly.

....

b Describe *two* ways in which you can prevent iron from rusting.

....

8Gc METALS AND WATER

1 Write word equations for the reactions of potassium and calcium with water.

a ....

....

b ....

....

2 Look at the diagram of four different metals reacting with cold water.

List the order of their reactivity (most reactive first).

....

A   B   C   D

3 The table shows a 'confidence grid'. Tick (✓) *one* box for each statement in the table.

Statement	Is definitely correct	Might be correct	Might be wrong	Is definitely wrong
a When a metal reacts with water, the only product is the metal hydroxide.				
b When metals react with oxygen, one product is always hydrogen.				
c Hydrogen gas in a boiling tube burns with a squeaky pop.				
d A catalyst needs to be regularly replaced as it gets used up.				

4 Look at the table. Use it to help identify the metals below.

a Metal X reacts in air but does not react with cold water.

Metal X is ....

b Metal Y catches fire with cold water and burns in air.

Metal Y is ....

c Metal Z does not react in cold water and reacts only slowly or partially in air. Metal Z could be ....

or ....

Metal	Reaction with oxygen in air	Reaction with cold water
potassium	🔥	🔥
sodium	🔥	✓✓✓
lithium	🔥	✓✓
calcium	🔥	✓✓
magnesium	🔥	✓
aluminium	✓✓✓	•••
zinc	✓✓	•••
iron	✓✓	•••
tin	✓	•••
lead	✓	•••
copper	✓	✗

Key

🔥 can catch fire	✓✓✓ reacts very quickly	✓✓ reacts quickly
✓ reacts	••• slow or partial reaction	✗ no reaction

1 Tick (✓) the correct ending for each sentence in parts **a** and **b** below.

a Accuracy describes:
- ☐ **A** how reliable a measurement is.
- ☐ **B** how close a measurement is to its real value.
- ☐ **C** how best to find the exact value of a measurement.
- ☐ **D** how to control all the variables in an experiment.

b An anomalous result is:
- ☐ **A** one that does not fit the pattern of other results.
- ☐ **B** produced when an experiment only gives you one reading.
- ☐ **C** one that you can be sure is correct.
- ☐ **D** one that you use to work out how accurate the rest of your results are.

2 Explain the difference between repeatable and reproducible data.

....

....

3 The drawing shows a 20 litre bucket, a 1 litre jug, a 500 cm³ beaker and a 50 cm³ measuring cylinder.

Identify the one that should be used to measure:

a the volume of drink left in a 330 cm³ can after a few sips have been drunk

....

b the volume of milk present in two nearly half full 1 litre bottles

....

c the volume of water in a sink.

....

4 Three groups of students added different metals (A, B and C) to hydrochloric acid. They recorded the volume of hydrogen gas produced by each. The tables show their results.

Student group X

	Volume of gas collected in 20 s (cm³)
Metal A	23

Student group Y

	Volume of gas collected in 20 s (cm³)
Metal B	28
Metal B	24
Metal B	26
Metal B	35

Student group Z

	Volume of gas collected in 20 s (cm³)
Metal C	50
Metal C	51
Metal C	52
Metal C	51

a Explain which group's data is the least reliable to use. _____

_____

b Explain which set of data has the most repeatable results. _____

_____

c Circle an anomalous reading.

d Suggest a reason for this anomalous reading.

_____

e State which metal is most reactive. _____

5a Make up a missing words exercise, where the words in the box are the ones that need filling in.

| accurate | anomalous | reliable | repeatable | reproducible |

_____

_____

_____

_____

b Try out your exercise with a friend and ask them for feedback. If you can, make improvements to your original exercise in a different colour.

1 When added to dilute acid, name a metal that might:

a explode _____   **b** not react. _____

2a Use a *pencil* to tick (✓) whether the statements below are true or false.

Statement	True	False
i Metals react faster with acids than with water.	☐	☐
ii If a metal reacts with an acid, effervescence occurs.	☐	☐
iii After a metal reacts with an acid, the metal is always visible in the solution.	☐	☐
iv If a metal and an acid react, the only product is hydrogen.	☐	☐
v A salt will catalyse reactions between acids and metals.	☐	☐

b Ask your teacher how many of your answers are correct. Then work with others and the Student Book to identify your incorrect answers. Make corrections and check with your teacher. Do this until they are all correct.

3 Calcium was added to hydrochloric acid until the reaction stopped. The diagram shows the final two stages in the preparation of a sample of the salt.

beaker

filter paper

filter funnel

conical flask

X

evaporating basin

gauze

tripod

heat

Y

a State what is happening in diagram X.

_____

b Give the reason why this is done.

_____

c State what is happening in diagram Y.

_____

d Give the reason why this is done.

_____

e Name the salt that has been prepared.

_____

4 Give the general equation for the reaction between a metal and an acid.

....

5 Complete the following equations.

a $Mg + H_2SO_4 \rightarrow MgSO_4 +$ ....

b $Ba + H_2SO_4 \rightarrow$ .... $+ H_2$

c iron + ... $\rightarrow$ iron chloride + hydrogen

d .... + nitric acid $\rightarrow$ sodium nitrate + ...

6a Complete the table below that gives information about metals reacting with acids and the salts they produce.

Metal	Acid	Salt (name)	Salt (symbols)	Ratio of different atoms in the salt
magnesium (Mg)	hydrochloric acid (HCl)	magnesium chloride	$MgCl_2$	1:2
sodium (Na)		sodium chloride		1:1
magnesium (Mg)			$MgSO_4$	1:1:4
potassium (K)	sulfuric acid (H_2SO_4)	potassium sulfate	K_2SO_4	
potassium (K)	nitric acid (HNO_3)			1:1:3

b Describe the test that will determine the gas produced in these reactions.

....

....

7 In your group, look at your answers to question **4** on page 75. Discuss your ideas again to find out if they have changed. Now, write a better answer in the lower box on that page.

8Ge PURE METALS AND ALLOYS

1a Explain the difference between a mixture and a pure substance.

....

b Use your answer to part **a** to help you describe what an alloy is.

....

....

2 Below is a table of information about different alloys of copper and iron.

Alloy	Composition	Properties compared to the main metal in the alloy
bronze	90% copper 10% tin	• harder • stronger • does not corrode easily • more shiny
brass	70% copper 30% zinc	• stronger • improved ductility (easily deformed) • more shiny
steel	99% iron 1% carbon	• harder • stronger
stainless steel	74% iron 18% chromium X% carbon	• stronger • more shiny • does not corrode

a Explain why sculptures in public parks are made from bronze rather than copper.

....

b Some musical instruments are made out of long lengths of brass tube. Why can brass be pulled into tube shapes more easily than copper?

....

c State a reason why stainless steel is used to make knives and forks but steel is not.

....

d Calculate the percentage of carbon in stainless steel.

....

e Name the property that all the alloys have that is an improvement over their pure metals.

....

3 The diagram shows a model of the atoms in a metal and an alloy.

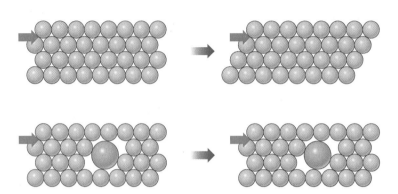

a Add labels to the diagram to explain why there is a difference in properties between the pure metal and the alloy, when a force is applied.

b Share your labels with others in your group. If you think you can improve your labelling, add any changes in a different colour.

4 Use a *pencil* to tick (✓) the correct ending for each sentence in parts **a** to **d** below.

a The melting point of a pure solid is the temperature at which:
- ☐ **A** it turns into another substance.
- ☐ **B** it turns into a liquid.
- ☐ **C** the atoms break all the bonds between them.
- ☐ **D** the atoms break apart.

b The boiling point of a pure liquid is the temperature at which:
- ☐ **A** the water in it evaporates.
- ☐ **B** it turns into a gas.
- ☐ **C** it becomes invisible.
- ☐ **D** evaporation occurs under its surface.

c Melting and boiling points are useful for identifying pure substances because:
- ☐ **A** those temperatures are fixed and do not change.
- ☐ **B** pure substances are always easy to melt and boil.
- ☐ **C** they occur at the same time.
- ☐ **D** they are the same value but one is positive and one is negative.

d The melting point of an alloy:
- ☐ **A** is the same as the melting point of the metal that the alloy contains the most of.
- ☐ **B** is fixed, and occurs at one certain temperature.
- ☐ **C** does not occur at one certain temperature but over a range of temperatures.
- ☐ **D** is the same as the boiling point of the metal that the alloy contains the least of.

5 Ask your teacher how many of your answers to question **4** are correct. Then work with others and the Student Book to identify your incorrect answers. Make corrections and check with your teacher. Do this until they are all correct.

1 Give the name of a scientist that studies metals.

....

2 The graph shows how the conductivity of an alloy of two metals, X and Y, varies with composition.

a You are a scientist looking for a material that can be used in the wiring for a car. State the best composition of the alloy for this use.

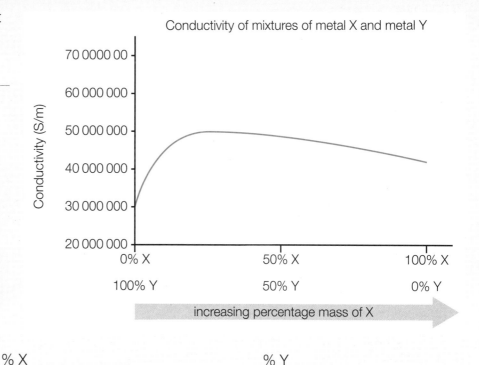

Conductivity of mixtures of metal X and metal Y

increasing percentage mass of X

.... % X   .... % Y

b At this composition, the alloy is not suitable. Suggest a property that it may have that makes it unsuitable for electrical wiring.

....

3 Work in a group to design a device that will test *one* of these properties: strength, ductility, malleability or heat conductivity.

a What property have you chosen? ....

b Is your device a new invention or will you adapt an existing device? ....

c Explain the main features of your design and how it will work by drawing a labelled diagram in the space below.

1 Drawings A–D show objects made of different metals.

A

C

B

a Suggest which metal you think each of objects A, B and C is made of.

A ....

B ....

C ....

b Suggest a suitable alloy for sculpture D.

D

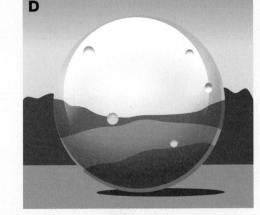

D ....

2 Write down the ratio of the different atoms in the following compounds.

a $MgCl_2$ ....
b NaOH ....
c $BaSO_4$ ....
d K_2SO_4 ....

3 Zinc is added to dilute hydrochloric acid and a reaction occurs. When copper is added the reaction rate increases (the reaction is speeded up).

a State the purpose of the copper in this process.

....

b State what will be left in the tube at the end of the reaction.

....

4 Complete the table below.

Metal	Reactant(s)	Product(s)
magnesium	water	magnesium hydroxide + hydrogen
iron	oxygen	
calcium		calcium hydroxide + hydrogen
copper	oxygen	
barium	hydrochloric acid	
iron	water + oxygen	
indium		indium nitrate + hydrogen

8Ha DISASTER

1a State *two* problems that can be caused when volcanoes erupt.

i ....   **ii** ....

b What is the name given to molten rock that spills out of a volcano? ....

2 Erupting volcanoes produce a lot of CO_2. What type of substance is carbon dioxide? Tick (✓) *one* box.

☐ **A** an element   ☐ **B** a mixture   ☐ **C** a compound   ☐ **D** an atom

3a What effect does carbon dioxide have on the temperature of the Earth?

....

b Name *one* human activity that adds carbon dioxide to the atmosphere.

....

4 When volcanoes erupt, sulfur dioxide, water vapour, and ash and rock fragments often enter the atmosphere.

a Give the name of a compound released during an eruption.

....

b Give the name of a mixture released during an eruption.

1 Complete the sentences using words from the box. Use each word only once.

compounds	grains	rocks	shapes	texture

_____ are mixtures of different minerals. The minerals are chemical

_____ and these form _____ that fit

together. The grains are different sizes and _____ and give the rock its

_____ .

2 Rocks made of rounded grains are said to be porous.

a What does the term porous mean?

_____

_____

b Draw a diagram in the box on the right to show how grains are arranged in a porous rock. Add labels to explain why the rock is porous.

c Name *one* type of porous rock.

_____

3 Limestone is a rock that is used in building.
Give *two* uses of limestone.

_____

_____

4a State the number of different minerals in the rock on the right.

_____

b Describe the grains in this rock.

_____

_____

1 mm

5 Suggest *two* important properties for a rock used to make:

a a statue _____

b a house. _____

8Hb IGNEOUS ROCKS

1 Label the diagram of the Earth.

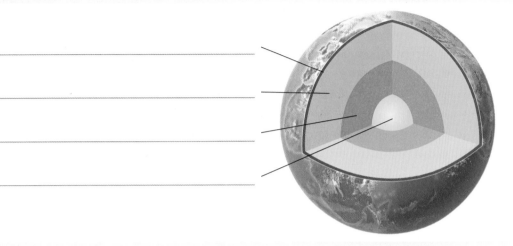

_____

_____

_____

_____

2 What is the difference between lava and magma?

3 Explain what happens to particles as liquid rock cools down. To answer this, tick (✓) *one* box for each of parts **a** and **b** below.

a As liquid rock cools down, the particles:
- ☐ **A** stop moving.
- ☐ **B** start to form a grid pattern.
- ☐ **C** start to get bigger.
- ☐ **D** start to get smaller.

b This is due to:
- ☐ **A** forces of attraction between the particles.
- ☐ **B** forces of repulsion between the particles.
- ☐ **C** the rock cooling down.
- ☐ **D** atoms combining to make them bigger.

4a Name an igneous rock.

b Some igneous rocks are intrusive (they form underground). Explain why intrusive igneous rocks have large crystals.

A
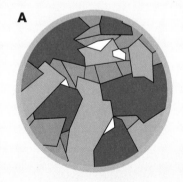

B
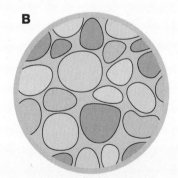

5a Which of the diagrams on the right is most likely to be extrusive rock? Tick (✓) *one*.

b Give a reason for your answer.

C
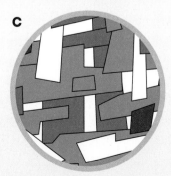

D
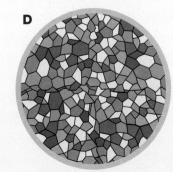

1 State the conditions in the Earth that lead to the formation of metamorphic rocks.

....

....

SB

2 Look at the diagram. At which of the numbered places will you find metamorphic rocks? Explain your answer.

....

....

....

....

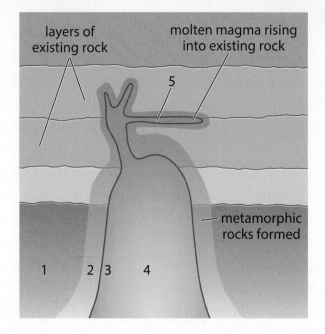

layers of existing rock

molten magma rising into existing rock

5

metamorphic rocks formed

1   2 3   4

3 Look at the drawings of granite, gneiss and basalt below.
a State which is the metamorphic rock.

....

b Give a reason for your answer.

....

A granite   **B** gneiss   **C** basalt

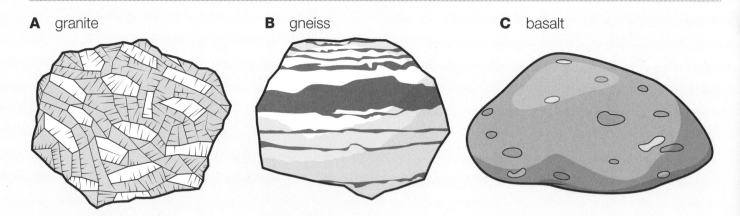

4 Read the following paragraph about the formation of different types of rocks. Underline or highlight the names of three different metamorphic rocks.

A rock called amphibolite is often found near basalt that has been found buried deep underground and heated to 700 °C or more. A rock called sandstone is formed from sand grains. Quartzite can be formed when sandstone is heated. Both quartzite and granite are very hard rocks. Gneiss resembles the granite it is formed from, with layers of coarse grains.

5 How confident are you at describing how igneous and metamorphic rocks are formed? Draw a smile on the face in the box to show how confident you are – the bigger the smile, the more confident you are.

1 Suggest why a volcano grows bigger before it erupts.

....

....

2 The diagram shows a model of a volcano. When vinegar (an acid) is poured into it, a chemical reaction occurs.

a State *one* way in which this is a good model of a volcano.

....

....

b State *one* way in which this is a poor model of a volcano.

....

....

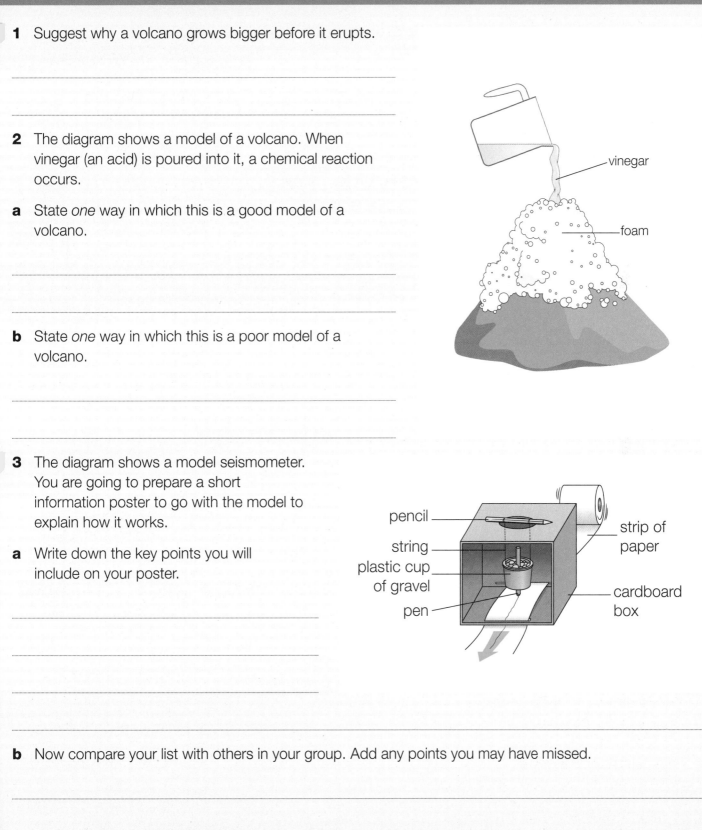

vinegar

foam

3 The diagram shows a model seismometer. You are going to prepare a short information poster to go with the model to explain how it works.

a Write down the key points you will include on your poster.

....

....

....

pencil

string

plastic cup of gravel

pen

strip of paper

cardboard box

b Now compare your list with others in your group. Add any points you may have missed.

....

....

8Hc WEATHERING AND EROSION

1 Draw *one* line from each type of weathering to one cause.

Type of weathering	Cause
biological weathering	due to temperature changes
chemical weathering	due to plants growing in cracks
physical weathering	due to acidic rain

2a Freeze–thaw action is a type of which sort of weathering? ....

b From the following list, tick (✔) which rocks are most likely to be affected by freeze–thaw action.

☐ granite   ☐ sandstone   ☐ limestone

☐ basalt   ☐ gneiss   ☐ marble

3 Air pollution can cause acid rain, which contains nitric acid and sulfuric acid. Complete the word equations to show the reactions of these acids with limestone (which is calcium carbonate).

a nitric acid + ... → .... nitrate + ... + carbon

....

b sulfuric acid + calcium carbonate → .... + ... +

....

c Write down *one* reactant from **a** or **b**. ....

d Write down *one* product from **a** or **b**. ....

4 The table shows a 'confidence grid'. Tick (✔) *one* box for each statement in the table.

Statement	Definitely correct	Might be correct	Might be wrong	Definitely wrong
Freeze–thaw action happens in wet places where the temperature often goes below 0 °C.				
Physical weathering only occurs when there is contact between a rock and water.				
Carbonates, such as limestone, react with acid and are used to make soils less acidic.				
Physical weathering is when bits of rock are moved from place to place.				

5 State the factor that determines the size of sediment particles that a stream can carry.

....

6 What happens to the shape of rocks that are transported in streams?

....

7 Glaciers can also cause abrasion.

a What is a glacier? ....

b Describe how glaciers cause abrasion. ....

....

....

8 The diagram shows how rocks are weathered by freeze–thaw action. Complete the labels below, to describe what happens at each stage (**a–d**).

a   **b**   **c**   **d**

a Water ....

b When the temperature goes below 0 °C ....

....

c When the temperature rises, water contracts as it ....

....

d Repeated expansion and ....

....

8Hd SEDIMENTARY ROCKS

1a The diagrams show the formation of a sedimentary rock. Use the words in the box to write captions for each stage (**i–iv**).

| cementation | compaction | sedimentation |

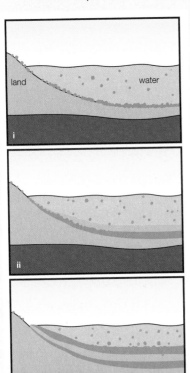

i ....

ii ....

iii ....

iv ....

b Compare your labelling to others in your group. Improve your labels if you can.

2 Sedimentary rocks can be turned into metamorphic rocks.

a What has to happen for a sedimentary rock to become a metamorphic one?

....

b Cross out the incorrect words to complete the sentences.

A sedimentary rock called *basalt / mudstone* can be turned into *marble / slate* by heat and pressure. In a similar way sandstone can be turned into *fossils / quartzite*.

3 Where does the 'glue' come from that holds the grains together in a sedimentary rock?

1 The flow chart summarises the scientific method.

State the term that is missing from the third box.

....

2 How does a scientific hypothesis becomes a theory?
Tick (✓) the *best* answer.

☐ **A** When you test the hypothesis, you get results that agree with it.

☐ **B** A scientist makes a hypothesis.

☐ **C** The data from many investigations support it.

☐ **D** An investigation gives identical results when carried out a second time.

3 Read the following statements about the scientific method. Tick (✓) those that you think are correct.

☐ **A** It is often impossible to control variables when doing geology investigations.

☐ **B** Geologists cannot do experiments and so do not use the scientific method.

☐ **C** Scientists can never prove that a hypothesis is true.

☐ **D** The data collected must be quantitative for a hypothesis to be true.

☐ **E** A prediction tells us what has happened in an experiment.

☐ **F** If a single test shows the prediction is correct, the hypothesis becomes a theory.

4 Draw a new version of the diagram above to show the scientific method for a geologist.

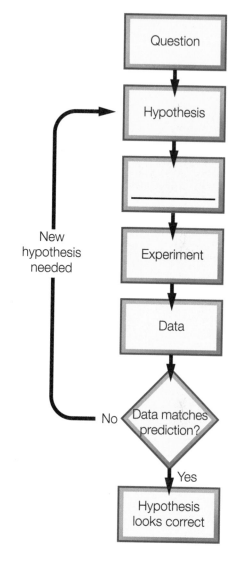

SB

1 How is investigating the Earth different from investigating chemical reactions or electricity?

2 The masses of pieces of granite, marble, sandstone and limestone were measured. The rocks were then put in water for two hours. After drying them, their masses were measured again. The mass of water absorbed per gram of rock was then calculated.

a State the independent variable.

b State the dependent variable.

c Describe the hypothesis being tested.

d Predict which rock would absorb most water.

e Explain how you came up with your prediction.

3 Jelly can be used as a model to help investigate how the runniness of the lava affects how far it will flow. The jelly is made more runny by adding more water. The results of one experiment are shown in the table.

a Give the independent variable.

Volume of hot water used to make jelly (cm³)	Time taken to travel 10 cm down a ramp (s)
5	42.0
8	37.0
10	20.2
12	10.3
15	15.4
20	10.5

b Suggest *two* control variables.

c State which result is anomalous.

d Describe what the results show.

1 Iron pyrite, also known as 'fool's gold', has the formula FeS_2.

a Tick (✓) *two* statements that are true.

- ☐ **A** Iron pyrite is a mineral.
- ☐ **B** The iron in iron pyrite is found in its native state.
- ☐ **C** FeS_2 is a compound.
- ☐ **D** Iron pyrite contains gold.
- ☐ **E** Iron pyrite contains three elements.
- ☐ **F** Gold is often found in sedimentary rocks.

b How confident are you that you chose both correct sentences? Write 0, 1 or 2 in the box.

> 0 – My answer was a complete guess.
> 1 – I think I have at least one correct.
> 2 – I am certain that I have both correct.

2 Complete the following sentences.

a A rock that is worth mining is called an ....

b These rocks are obtained by ....

c The rocks are crushed to obtain the .... (which contain the metals).

d Metals that are found as elements are in their .... state.

3 State *two* ways in which mining can harm the environment.

....

....

4 Why don't all mine owners take steps to reduce pollution from their mines?

....

....

5 Describe *two* benefits of recycling smart phones.

....

....

1a Label the rock cycle in the diagram. Draw a line from each bullet point in the left-hand list to a bullet point in a box or on an arrow.

b In the boxes on the diagram, write in one example of each different type of rock.

c Compare your labels with others. Make any corrections or additions in a different colour.

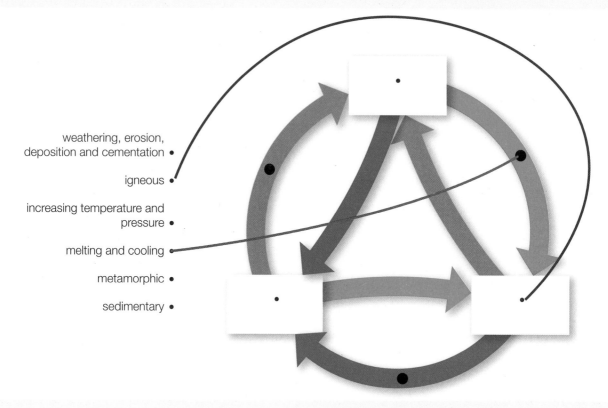

weathering, erosion, deposition and cementation •

igneous •

increasing temperature and pressure •

melting and cooling •

metamorphic •

sedimentary •

2 Explain how magma can form either basalt (with small crystals) or gabbro (with large crystals).

3 If a volcano stopped erupting, it would eventually get smaller.

a Describe *two* ways in which the rocks could be weathered.

b Describe *two* ways in which the weathered fragments could be transported.

4 Limestone (calcium carbonate) reacts with sulfuric acid. Complete the word equation for this reaction.

calcium carbonate + sulfuric acid →   + water +

8Ia EXPLORING EXTREMES

1 Matter can exist as a solid, liquid or gas. Which state of matter is:

a snow ....

b air ....

c water in the ocean? ....

2 A few explorers have visited the deepest parts of the oceans, 11 km below the surface. Their submarines withstand forces 1000 times bigger than on the surface.

a Explain in as much detail as you can:

i what causes the forces on the outside of a submarine ....

....

ii why the forces are much greater at the bottom of the ocean than they are at sea level.

....

....

b Suggest *two* other problems people have to overcome to visit the bottom of the sea.

....

....

3 Mountaineers have also visited the highest mountains in the world. The top of Mount Everest is nearly 9 km above sea level.

a Most climbers use oxygen masks when they climb this high. Explain, in as much detail as you can, why

they need to do this. ....

....

b Suggest *two* other problems that people have to overcome when climbing high mountains.

....

....

4 You may not have known all the answers to questions **2** and **3**. Work with a partner to write a list of things you need to find out about to help you write better answers to these questions.

....

....

1 What property do solids and liquids share and why? Tick (✓) *one* box for each of parts **a** and **b** below.

a Solids and liquids both:
- ☐ **A** have fixed shapes.
- ☐ **B** are difficult to compress.
- ☐ **C** flow.
- ☐ **D** fill the container they are in.

b This is because the particles in them:
- ☐ **A** vibrate about fixed positions.
- ☐ **B** are different sizes.
- ☐ **C** are very close together.
- ☐ **D** are held together by very strong forces.

2 Explain why solids and liquids behave differently. Tick (✓) *one* box for each of parts **a** and **b** below.

a A property that is very different between solids and liquids is:
- ☐ **A** having a fixed volume.
- ☐ **B** having a fixed mass.
- ☐ **C** being able to be compressed.
- ☐ **D** having a fixed shape.

b This is different because:
- ☐ **A** the forces between particles are stronger in liquids than in solids.
- ☐ **B** the forces between particles are stronger in solids than in liquids.
- ☐ **C** the particles are closer together in liquids than in solids.
- ☐ **D** the particles in solids do not move.

3a Describe *one* similarity between the properties of liquids and gases.

....

b Describe *two* differences. ....

....

4a Draw *one* line from each scientific term to its correct definition.

Scientific term	**Definition**
Brownian motion	materials changing size when heated or cooled
diffusion	liquids or gases mixing without anything moving them
expanding and contracting	tiny specks in air or water jiggling around

b Use ideas about particles to explain why each of these things happens.

i Diffusion happens because ....

....

ii Brownian motion happens because ....

....

iii Materials expand when they are heated because ....

B **5** A substance cools down when energy is transferred away from it. Explain how this affects:

a the movement of the particles ....

....

b the size of the object. ....

....

6 Complete these sentences using words from the box.

| bigger | heated | liquid | mass | move around | smaller | vibrate | volume |

When a .... or gas is heated, the particles ....

faster and so need more space in which to move. When a solid is .... the

particles .... more and so the solid takes up more space.

Density is the mass of a certain .... of a material. When a material is heated

its .... does not change but the volume gets ....

This makes the density ....

B **7** Explain how a liquid thermometer works.

....

....

....

....

8 A bridge is built without expansion gaps. Explain what could happen to the bridge if the temperature became:

a much hotter than the day it was built ....

....

b much colder than the day it was built. ....

....

1 Density cannot be measured directly. Write down *two* quantities that you need to measure to allow you to calculate density.

....

2 Complete these sentences by crossing out the incorrect words.

The density of a liquid *decreases / increases* when it is heated. This happens because the liquid *contracts / expands*, so its volume *increases / decreases*. The mass does not change, but the *larger / smaller* volume means its density is now *greater / less* than before.

SB   **3** A piece of metal is a cuboid with width 2 cm, length 5 cm and height 1.5 cm. Calculate its volume.

SB   **4** Describe how to measure the volume of a piece of modelling clay.

....

....

5 Write down *two* different units used for:

a volume ....

b mass ....

c density. ....

6 The formula for calculating density can be written as $d = \dfrac{m}{v}$.

A student has a piece of material with a volume of 90 cm³ and a mass of 1.8 kg.

a Explain what they need to do to calculate the density in g/cm³.

....

b Calculate the density.

density = ... unit ....

8Ia CALCULATIONS WITH DENSITY (WS)

7 This triangle helps you to calculate the density, volume or mass.

Write down the equations that you need to use to calculate:

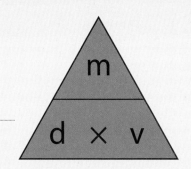

a mass, if you are given a density and a volume

_____

b volume, if you are given a density and a mass.

....

8a Calculate the missing values in this table. Write your answers in pencil.

	Mass	Volume	Density	Unit
i	10 g	40 cm³		
ii	50 kg	2 m³		
iii	0.4 kg	20 cm³		
iv	90 kg		30	kg/m³
v		4 cm³	40	g/cm³
vi	81 g		27	g/cm³
vii		8 m³	50	kg/m³

b Ask your teacher to check how many of your answers are correct. Work with a partner and the Student Book to identify your incorrect answers. Make corrections and check with your teacher. Do this until they are all correct.

9 The density of aluminium is 2.7 g/cm³. You have a piece of aluminium with a volume of 50 cm³.

a Write down the formula you need to use to calculate its mass.

....

b Work out its mass.

mass = _____ g

c Calculate the volume of 810 g of aluminium.

volume = _____ unit _____

8Ib CHANGING STATE

1 Explain why diffusion is a physical change. _____

2a Name *two* other physical changes. _____

b Name *two* chemical changes. _____

3 The graph shows how the temperature changes as a pure substance is cooled and then heated again.

a Add the following labels to the graph. One has been done for you.

    B where the substance is boiling
    C where it is condensing
    F where it is freezing
    G where it is a gas
    L where it is a liquid
    M where is it melting
    S where it is solid

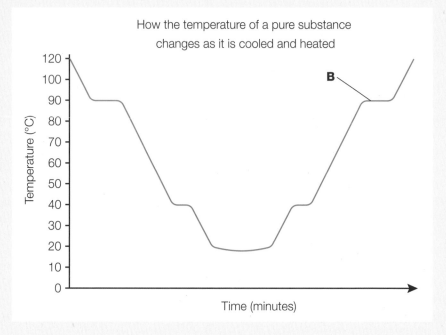

How the temperature of a pure substance changes as it is cooled and heated

b Compare your answers to part **a** with a partner to check for mistakes. Mark any corrections to your labels in a different colour.

4a What is the melting point of the substance? Draw a horizontal line across the graph to help you to work out the answer. _____

b What is the boiling point of the substance? _____

c What is the freezing point of the substance? _____

d Explain why you do not need the graph to work out your answer to part **c**. _____

5a Explain why there is no such thing as an evaporation point.

_____

b What happens to a substance when it sublimes?

6 The graph shows how the volume of a substance changes as it is heated. Describe what the graph shows.

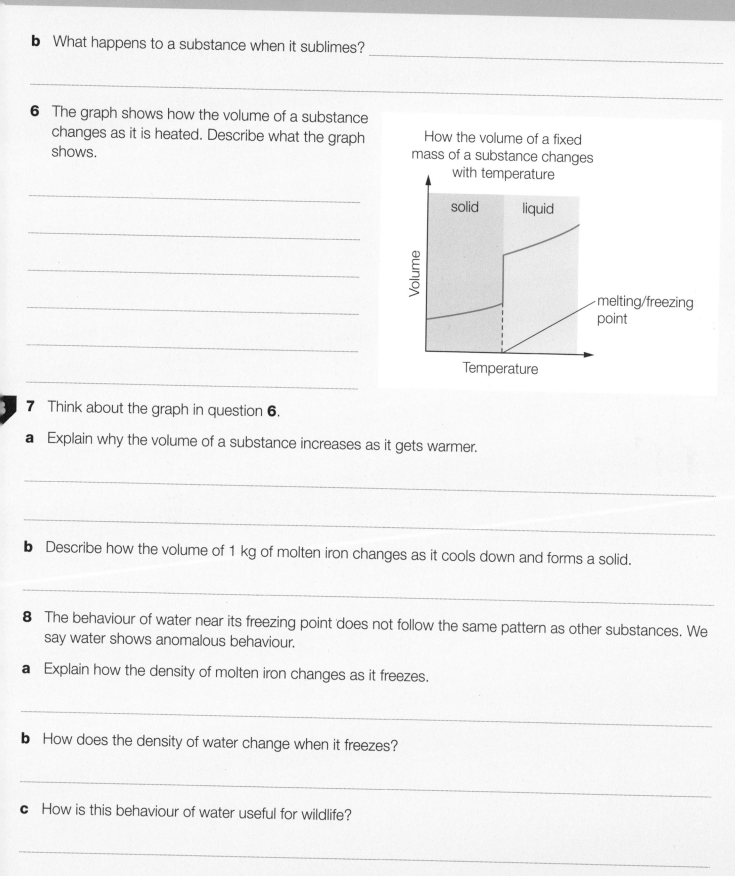

How the volume of a fixed mass of a substance changes with temperature

solid   liquid

Volume

melting/freezing point

Temperature

7 Think about the graph in question **6**.

a Explain why the volume of a substance increases as it gets warmer.

b Describe how the volume of 1 kg of molten iron changes as it cools down and forms a solid.

8 The behaviour of water near its freezing point does not follow the same pattern as other substances. We say water shows anomalous behaviour.

a Explain how the density of molten iron changes as it freezes.

b How does the density of water change when it freezes?

c How is this behaviour of water useful for wildlife?

1 What is a fluid? ....

SB

2 What causes pressure in fluids? ....

....

3 Why do we not notice the pressure of the air around us?

....

....

4 Explain how the air pressure inside a bicycle tyre compares to the air pressure outside. To answer this, tick (✔) *one* box for each of parts **a** and **b** below.

a The air pressure inside the tyre is:
- ☐ **A** higher.
- ☐ **B** the same.
- ☐ **C** lower.
- ☐ **D** zero.

b This is because:
- ☐ **A** the air inside the tyre is colder.
- ☐ **B** more air particles have been put into the tyre.
- ☐ **C** the particles in the tyre are moving faster.
- ☐ **D** the air inside the tyre is warmer.

5 Explain how the air pressure changes as you go down a deep mine. To answer this, tick (✔) *one* box for each of parts **a** and **b** below.

a The air pressure:
- ☐ **A** decreases.
- ☐ **B** stays the same.
- ☐ **C** increases.
- ☐ **D** stays the same.

b This is because:
- ☐ **A** there is more atmosphere above you.
- ☐ **B** the air particles are hitting you harder.
- ☐ **C** the air particles in the mine are moving faster.
- ☐ **D** the air inside the mine is colder.

SB

6 If you take a sealed bag of potato snacks up a mountain, the bag expands. Explain why this happens, using ideas about particles and pressure.

....

....

....

7 In a group, discuss your answers to question **6** and check the Student Book. Work together to write a better answer. Copy it onto the lines below.

....

....

....

....

1 The drawing shows a hot air balloon floating at a constant height. There are two forces on it.

Draw a force arrow to show the missing force. Label both arrows.

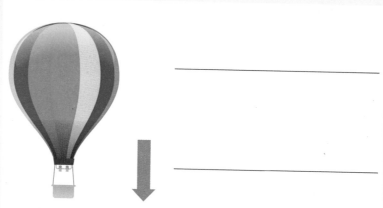

2a What *two* forces affect you when you float?

b How do these two forces compare in size?

3 Look at the diagram of four different blocks of material in water.

a Write the density of the water and of each material in the correct places. Choose your answers from the densities in the box.

| 0.05 | 0.4 | 0.8 | 1.0 | 2.0 |

b Ask your teacher how many you have got correct. Work with a partner and the Student Book to identify your incorrect answers. Make corrections and check with your teacher. Do this until they are all correct.

c Explain how you worked out your answers to part **a**.

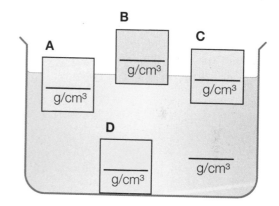

d Is there any upthrust on block D? Explain your answer.

4 Iron has a density of 8 g/cm³ and polystyrene has a density of 0.01 g/cm³.

a Explain whether a cube of iron will float in mercury (the density of mercury is 13.6 g/cm³).

b Explain why polystyrene will float in water but not in air.

8Ie DRAG

1 What is drag? ....

2a Part of the drag on an object is caused by friction.

i How does friction change the object (apart from slowing it down)?

....

ii How is the friction part of the drag reduced?

....

b Part of the drag is caused because the object has to push some of the fluid out of the way.

i Explain how the speed of the object affects this part of the drag.

....

....

ii Describe *one* way to reduce this part of the drag.

....

3 The drawings show two forces on a car as it accelerates to top speed. Complete the drawings by adding force arrows to show how the drag changes as the car goes faster. The first one has been done for you.

just starting off   still accelerating   top speed

4a Suggest *two* ways in which a car designer could increase the top speed of a new car.

i ....

ii ....

b Explain why each way works, using ideas about balanced forces.

i ....

....

ii ....

....

5 Draw a smile on the face to show your confidence in your answers to question **4** – the bigger the smile, the more confident you are.

8Ie OPERATING AEROPLANES (STEM)

1a Explain why maps used by pilots have internationally agreed symbols. ....

....

b Write down the internationally recognised unit for density. ....

c There are international standards for the colours of wires in electrical appliances. Explain why it is important to follow these standards.

....

....

2 The graph shows how air density changes with height. Air density also depends on temperature. Hot air is less dense than cold air.

Compare the density of the air at 12 km with the density at sea level.

How air density changes with height

3 Explain how the lift from a wing changes when an aeroplane:

a slows down ....

b climbs to a greater height. ....

....

4 Explain why an aeroplane has a higher take-off speed on a hot day.

....

....

HUMANS AT THE EXTREMES

1 Look back at your answer to question **4** on page 99.

a How many of the things have you found out while studying this unit?

....

....

b Use your new knowledge to help you to answer questions **2** and **3** below, then compare them to your answers on page 99.

2 A few explorers have visited the deepest parts of the oceans, 11 km below the surface. Their submarines withstand forces 1000 times bigger than on the surface. Explain in as much detail as you can:

a what causes the forces on the outside of a submarine

....

....

b why the forces are much greater at the bottom of the ocean than they are at sea level.

....

....

3 Mountaineers have also visited the highest mountains in the world. The top of Mount Everest is nearly 9 km above sea level. Most climbers use oxygen masks when they climb this high. Explain, in as much detail as you can, why they need to do this.

....

....

4 A submarine is designed to go as fast as possible.

a Describe *three* ways in which the drag can be kept small for a given speed.

....

....

b The submarine has tanks that can be filled with air or water. Explain why filling the tanks with water makes the overall density of the submarine increase.

....

....

8Ja SEEING THINGS

1 Draw *one* line from each scientific term to its correct definition.

Scientific term	Definition
light source	a material that light can travel through without scattering
transparent	a material that does not let light through
shadow	a place that light cannot reach because something is blocking it
opaque	something that produces light

2 Explain why you can see an image of yourself in a mirror, but not if you look at a sheet of paper. Tick (✓) *one* box.

- ☐ **A** Paper has a smoother surface than a mirror.
- ☐ **B** A mirror reflects light evenly but paper scatters it.
- ☐ **C** Paper reflects light evenly but a mirror scatters it.
- ☐ **D** Paper is opaque and a mirror is not.

3a You are watching a light show across a lake. Buildings have lights on them, and laser beams shine into the sky. Write a paragraph to explain how you can see the buildings and the water.

b Explain how you can see the laser beams in the light show.

c Compare your answer to part **b** with others in your group. Are there any parts you do not agree on? Have you missed out anything?

d Write a list of things you need to find out about to help you to write a better answer.

8Ja LIGHT ON THE MOVE

1 Write the correct scientific term next to each definition.

.... to take in

.... to pass through a substance

.... to bounce off a surface

.... to send things off in different directions

2 In a thunderstorm, you see the flash of lighting before you hear the thunder. Give the reason why this happens.

....

....

3 Light and sound both travel as waves. Write down two differences between light waves and sound waves.

i ....

ii ....

4 Add light rays to the drawings to show how the boy can see a programme on TV, and how the girl can read a book.

SB

5 Look at the diagram.

Which material (X, Y or Z) is:

a translucent ....

b opaque? ....

c Explain your answers.

....

6 Someone is singing in another room with the door closed. Explain why you can hear them but not see them.

....

....

7 The diagram shows a box standing next to a light source.

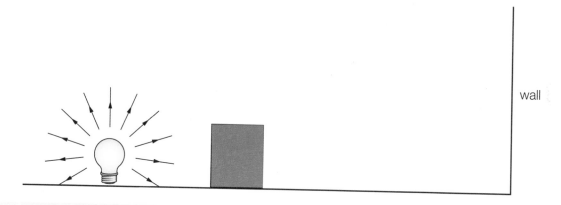

a Explain why the box makes a shadow on the wall.

....

b Finish drawing one of the rays to work out where the top of the shadow will be. Shade in the shadowed part of the wall.

c The box is moved closer to the wall. Draw lines on the diagram to help you to work out the new size of the shadow.

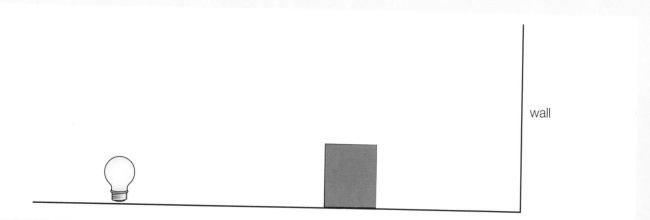

d Draw a smile on the face to show how confident you are that your answers to parts **a** to **c** are correct – the bigger the smile, the more confident you are.

SB **1** Why do we need to use ray boxes and paper when we investigate light?

....

....

SB **2** Why is it important to use agreed symbols and conventions in science?

....

....

3a Draw *one* line from each scientific term to its correct definition.

Scientific term	Definition
angle of incidence	a diagram showing rays of light as straight lines with arrows showing which way the light is going
angle of reflection	a flat mirror
incident ray	a line drawn at right angles to the mirror
normal	a ray of light travelling away from the mirror after being reflected
plane mirror	a ray of light travelling towards a mirror
ray diagram	the angle between the incident ray and the normal
reflected ray	the angle between the reflected ray and the normal

b The diagram shows light being reflected by a mirror.

i Complete the diagram using the standard conventions for ray diagrams.

ii Label your diagram using words from part **a**.

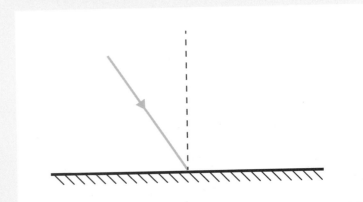

4a Write a set of instructions for investigating what happens to a ray of light when it hits a mirror.

Apparatus

Instructions

b Share your instructions with others. Discuss which instructions are best and why. On the lines below, write an improved version of *one* of your instructions.

c How have you improved this instruction?

5 A lens is fitted to the ray box to make the ray of light narrower and brighter. Explain how this can help to give more accurate results in this investigation.

SB 1 Light hits a plane mirror with an angle of incidence of 20°. What will the angle of reflection be? _____

2 These statements are about different kinds of reflection. Tick (✓) the boxes to show whether each one is true or false. Draw a smile on the face for each statement to show your confidence—the bigger the smile, the more confident you are.

Statement	True	False	
a Transparent materials do not reflect any light.	☐	☐	😐
b The law of reflection states that the angle of incidence is equal to the angle of reflection.	☐	☐	😐
c Smooth surfaces like mirrors produce diffuse reflection.	☐	☐	😐
d Rough surfaces scatter reflected light in all directions.	☐	☐	😐
e Paper produces diffuse reflection.	☐	☐	😐
f Specular reflection is when all the reflected rays of light go off in the same direction.	☐	☐	😐

SB 3 Explain why you can see your reflection better in a piece of metal if you polish the surface.

_____

_____

4a Complete the ray diagram below to show how we can see the reflection of a candle in a mirror. (*Hint*: You need to draw *two* rays and a dashed line.)

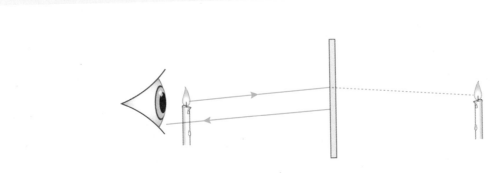

b Write 'image' next to the image on the diagram.

5a How big is the image in a plane mirror compared to the object being reflected? Tick (✔) *one* box.

☐ **A** The image is smaller than the object.
☐ **B** The image is the same size as the object.
☐ **C** The image is larger than the object.
☐ **D** The object is larger than the image.

b How far behind the mirror does the image appear to be? Tick (✔) *one* box.
☐ **A** The image appears further away from the mirror than the object.
☐ **B** The image appears closer to the mirror than the object.
☐ **C** The image appears the same distance from the mirror as the object.
☐ **D** The distance depends on the kind of object being reflected.

6 Hani says: 'The law of reflection works on all surfaces, even when the surface scatters light.'

a Explain why Hani is correct. You may refer to the diagram in your answer.

....

....

....

....

b Compare your answers to part **a** with a partner. Work together to improve your answers. Write your improved answer below.

....

....

....

....

1 Label the diagram on the right using words from the box.

angle of incidence   angle of refraction   normal

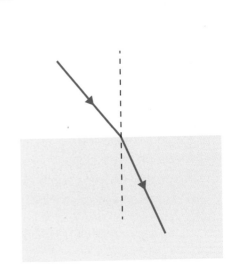

2 Complete these sentences by crossing out the incorrect words.

Refraction happens when light travels from one *opaque / transparent* substance to another.
It occurs when light travels from air into glass because light travels more *quickly / slowly* in glass or water than in air.

When a ray of light enters glass, it changes direction *away from / towards* the normal. When it goes from glass to air, it bends *away from / towards* the normal.

3 Diagrams X and Y show a ray of light going from glass to air, and from water to air. Finish drawing the light rays.

4 When you look into water in a swimming pool, objects on the bottom often appear to be closer to you than they really are. Explain why this happens.

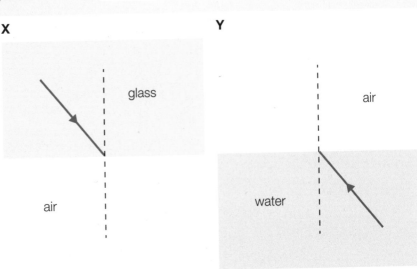

....

....

SB 5 Describe the shape of a converging lens. ....

....

6a Describe what a converging lens does to a beam of light. ....

....

b Explain how the thickness of a converging lens affects the position of the focal point of the lens.

8Jd CAMERAS AND EYES

1 The diagram shows a human eye.

a Write the correct letter next to each part of the eye.

i cornea ....

ii iris ....

iii lens ....

iv muscles ....

v optic nerve ....

vi pupil ....

vii retina ....

b Which part (or parts) of the eye:

i focuses light ....

ii lets light enter the eye ....

iii detects light and produces nerve impulses ....

iv helps the eye to focus on objects at different distances. ....

c Ask your teacher how many of your answers to parts **a** and **b** are correct. Then work with others and the Student Book to identify your incorrect answers. Make corrections and check with your teacher. Do this until they are all correct.

2 The iris can change the size of the pupil.

a How does the size of the pupil change when there is only dim light? ....

b Explain how this helps the person to see. ....

....

3 In a camera, electronic sensors detect light and produce electrical signals. Describe *one* difference between the electrical signals produced by a digital camera and an eye.

....

....

4 Name the primary colours of light. ....

SB **1** Explain why optometrists need to have good communication skills.

_____

_____

2 Look at the diagrams below.

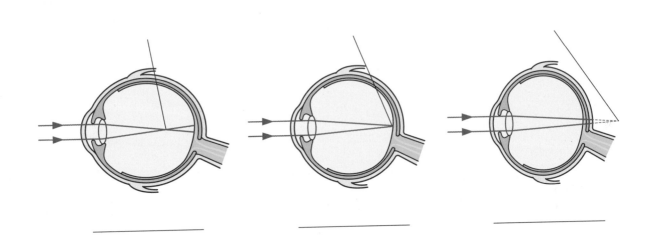

a Label the diagrams using words and phrases from the box.

> long sight   light focused on retina   light focused in front of retina
>
> light focused behind retina   normal vision   short sight

b The diagram above is to be used on an information poster for an optometrist's office. Write a short paragraph for the poster to explain the causes of long sight and short sight.

_____

_____

_____

_____

SB **3** A person can only read the top three rows on an optometrists' chart from 6 m away. Explain whether they are short sighted or long sighted.

_____

8Je COLOUR

1 Complete these sentences using words from the box.

dispersion	frequency	refracted	spectrum	water	white

Rainbows form when _____ drops in the air split up

_____ light into the different colours of the _____.

We can also split up white light using a prism, because each _____ of light is

_____ by different amounts. This effect is called _____.

2 The diagram shows white light passing through a prism. Violet light has the highest frequency of all the colours that make up white light.

a Explain how you can work out the relationship between the frequency of a ray of light and its angle of refracton.

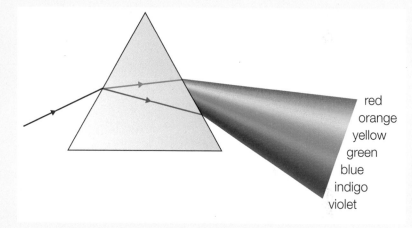

red
orange
yellow
green
blue
indigo
violet

_____

_____

b Share your explanation with others. Discuss how clear it is. Write down *one* thing you could improve

about your explanation. _____

_____

3 Which colours in white light does a blue object:

a reflect _____   **b** absorb? _____

4 Explain how a blue filter makes blue light.

_____

_____

5 Blue light shines on a red ball. Explain why the ball appears to be black.

_____

8Je INVISIBILITY CLOAKS

SB

1a What is the name of the process that bends light? _____

b When does this normally happen? _____

_____

2 Look back at your answer to question **3d** on page 111.

a How many of the things have you found out while studying this unit?

_____

_____

b Use your new knowledge to help you to answer question **3** below, then compare them to your answer to question **3b** on page 111.

3 Explain why you can see laser beams in a light show.

_____

_____

_____

4 You can use a lens to focus light to a point. Explain what happens to the light as it enters and leaves the glass lens.

_____

_____

_____

5 Explain why shining white light through a prism produces a spectrum.

_____

_____

_____

_____

SB **6** List the parts of your eye. _____

_____

1 Write down *four* different ways in which energy can be:

a transferred ....

....

b stored. ....

....

2 Explain the difference between evaporation and boiling.

....

....

....

3 Tick (✓) the boxes to show ways in which energy can be transferred by heating through the different materials. Some materials may have more than one tick.

	Conduction	Convection	Radiation
a opaque solids (e.g. metals)	☐	☐	☐
b opaque liquids (e.g. milk)	☐	☐	☐
c transparent gases (e.g. air)	☐	☐	☐
d transparent solids (e.g. glass)	☐	☐	☐
e empty space	☐	☐	☐

4 Answer these questions as best you can.

a Describe how energy is transferred through solid materials such as metals.

....

....

b Describe how energy is transferred through fluids (liquids and gases).

....

....

5 What do we mean when we say that one machine is more powerful than another?

....

....

8Ka TEMPERATURE CHANGES

1 What is the difference between internal energy and temperature?

_____

_____

2 Which of these factors affects the amount of internal energy stored in an object? Tick (✓) *three* boxes.

☐ its volume   ☐ its mass   ☐ the material it is made from

☐ its shape   ☐ its temperature   ☐ its colour

3 Look at the drawing.

a Which contains the greater mass of water: the kettle or the mug?

_____

b Is the water in the kettle or mug storing the greater amount of energy? Explain your answer.

_____

c Why do you think it takes longer to boil a kettle full of water than to boil only enough to fill the mug?

_____

250 cm³ of boiling water

1800 cm³ of boiling water

4 Look at the drawing of the mug in question **3**. Explain what will happen to the energy stored in the hot water and in the air in the room. To answer this question, tick (✓) *one* box for each of parts **a** and **b**.

a The energy stored in the hot water will:
- ☐ **A** evaporate.
- ☐ **B** remain unchanged.
- ☐ **C** be transferred to the air in the room.
- ☐ **D** increase as energy is transferred from the air in the room.

b This happens because:
- ☐ **A** of the law of conservation of energy.
- ☐ **B** energy flows from hotter things to cooler things.
- ☐ **C** energy flows from cooler things to hotter things.
- ☐ **D** the high temperature changes the energy in the mug.

5 An ice cube is left in a room at 21 °C for 10 hours.

a Explain what happens to it.

_____

_____

b Compare your answer to part **a** with a partner to check for mistakes. Make any corrections to your answer in a different colour.

1 Draw *one* line from each scientific term to its correct definition.

absorb

a material that allows internal (thermal) energy to be transferred through it easily

emit

a way of transferring energy by heating that does not need a material

infrared radiation

a material that does not allow internal (thermal) energy to be transferred through it easily

medium

any substance through which something travels

reflect

to give out

thermal conductor

to bounce off a surface (instead of passing through it or being absorbed)

thermal insulator

to take in

2 Describe *three* ways in which infrared radiation and light are similar.

_____

_____

3a Tick (✓) the boxes to show which statements are true and which are false. Draw a smiley face to show how confident you are in your answers.

Statement	True	False	
i Infrared radiation does not need a medium to travel through.	☐	☐	☺
ii Infrared radiation cannot travel through solids.	☐	☐	☺
iii Conduction happens better in liquids or gases than in solids.	☐	☐	☺
iv Conduction transfers energy by passing on vibrations between particles.	☐	☐	☺
v Metals are good thermal conductors.	☐	☐	☺
vi Hot objects emit more infrared radiation than cool ones.	☐	☐	☺

b Ask your teacher how many you have correct. Then work with others and the Student Book to identify your incorrect answers. Make changes and check with your teacher. Do this until they are all correct.

4 Explain why saucepans are usually made from metal but often have wooden or plastic handles?

_____

1 What is a fluid? ....

2 Look at the drawing of a room. The stove contains a fire.

stove

a Write a D on the drawing where the air becomes less dense than the air in the rest of the room.

b Explain your answer to part **a**. ....
....

c Draw an arrow to show how this less dense air moves.

d Draw more arrows in a different colour to show how a convection current will flow around the room. Label your arrows using phrases from the box.

> air cools down and sinks
>
> air pushed out of the way by rising warm air
>
> cooler air moves in to replace rising air

3a Why will cold air sink if it is surrounded by warmer air?

....

....

b Add arrows to the diagram of the ice lolly to show the direction of the convection currents caused by the cold lolly.

8Kc CONTROLLING TRANSFERS

1a Explain why air is a poor thermal conductor. ....

....

b Explain why air needs to be trapped to make a good thermal insulator. ....

....

....

2 How does insulating houses reduce energy use in cold countries? ....

....

....

3 The diagram shows a solar water heater.

a Draw arrows on the water pipes to show which way water flows through the heater.

b Explain how you worked out your answer to part **a**.

....

....

....

c Explain how the water heater is designed to absorb as much solar energy as possible.

copper pipes
painted black

insulated box
with glass top

water pipes

....

....

....

....

4 A black car and a white car are parked next to each other on a sunny day. Explain which car will:

a become hotter inside ....

b cool down faster at night. ....

5 Sweat helps to cool your body. Complete these sentences using words from the box to explain this.

| absorb | cooler | energy | evaporates | fastest | less | particles |

The .... in liquid sweat have different amounts of

.... The ones that move the .... escape

first when the sweat .... The particles that are left behind have

.... energy, and so the remaining liquid is ....

This cooler sweat can .... more energy from your body.

1 Complete the sentences using words from the box.

| accurate | precise | random | systematic | valid |

A set of results are _____ when repeated results are all close to the same

value. The results are _____ when they are close to the true value. Errors

that make all results incorrect by the same amount are called _____ errors.

_____ errors can make some results too high or too low. Your conclusion is

_____ if it relates to the original question and uses good quality data.

2 The following statements are about obtaining *accurate* results. Tick (✓) the boxes to show whether each is an advantage or disadvantage.

		Advantage	Disadvantage
a	Provide good quality data to help reach a valid conclusion.	☐	☐
b	May be difficult to obtain.	☐	☐
c	May need more expensive instruments.	☐	☐
d	Results are close to the true value of what is being measured.	☐	☐

3 These archery targets show where different people's arrows went. They were all aiming for the centre of the target.

A   B   C   D

a Write the correct letter next to each description of the archer's performance. One has been done for you. Show how confident you are in your answers by drawing smiles on the faces – the bigger the smile, the more confident you are.

	accurate but not precise
B	precise but not accurate
	accurate and precise
	neither accurate nor precise

b Explain why the archer's results in B were precise but not accurate.

4 Sunita is planning an investigation to find the melting points of four different types of wax.

Davinda is planning how to investigate whether body temperature increases after exercise.

Explain which thermometer each person should use.

| **Thermometer X** |
| Range: 35–42 °C Divisions 0.1 °C |
| **Thermometer Y** |
| Range: −10–110 °C Divisions 1 °C |

Sunita should use thermometer _____ because _____

_____

Davinda should use thermometer _____ because _____

5a On the right are the results obtained when different students measured the time it took to boil the same volume of water using a Bunsen burner.

What can you say about the precision of these results? _____

| 10.5 minutes 10.4 minutes |
| 10.5 minutes 10.5 minutes |
| 10.6 minutes |

b In the same investigation, measurements from the whole class were used to work out a mean time for heating of 10.9 minutes. Explain what this tells you about the accuracy of the results in part **a**.

6 Sally wants to measure how much a 15 cm long brass rod expands when she heats one end using a Bunsen burner. Ben is measuring how far water will rise up a thin tube when it is heated. Explain who will need to use the most accurate measuring instrument.

7 Share your answers to question **6** with other students. Work together to develop a better answer. Write your new answer below.

SB

1 What is the power rating of an electric shower transferring 10 000 J/s:

a in watts ....

b in kilowatts? ....

SB

2 An electric kettle has a power rating of 3 kW.

a How much energy does it transfer each second? ....

b Suggest why the kettle has a lower power rating than an electric shower.

---

3 Look at these labels from three electric kettles.

Explain which kettle will boil 1 litre of water the fastest. To answer this, tick (✓) *one* box for each of parts **a** and **b** below.

Model: X300	**Model: Y100**	**Model: Z5923**
230V~50 Hz	2500 W 230~50Hz	110V~50 Hz
1500 W		2200 W

a For these kettles:
- ☐ **A** they will take the same time.
- ☐ **B** the X300 will boil the water fastest.
- ☐ **C** the Y100 will boil the water fastest.
- ☐ **D** the Z5923 will boil the water fastest.

b This is because:
- ☐ **A** the Z5923 will transfer more energy because it needs a lower voltage.
- ☐ **B** the Y100 has a higher power rating and transfers more energy to the water each second.
- ☐ **C** the X300 has a higher power rating and transfers more energy to the water each second.
- ☐ **D** the Z5923 has a higher power rating and transfers more energy to the water each second.

4 The Sankey diagram shows the energy transfers in an electric kettle.

a How much energy is wasted by the kettle each second?

2000 J supplied each second by electricity

400 J transferred to the kettle and the surroundings

1600 J transferred to the water in the kettle by heating

....

b Calculate the efficiency of the kettle.

$$\text{efficiency} = \frac{\text{useful energy transferred}}{\text{total energy supplied}} \times 100\%$$

efficiency = ... %

c Suggest why it is more efficient to boil water in a kettle than in a saucepan. ....

---

5 A modern efficient light bulb transfers 9 J of energy by light every second. It uses 20 J of energy to do this.

a Calculate its efficiency.

efficiency = _____ %

b Sketch and label a Sankey diagram to show the energy transfers in the light bulb.

6 Students are comparing the efficiency of three different motors.

- Motor A uses 20 J of energy and transfers 15 J as useful energy.

- Motor B uses 50 J of energy and transfers 40 J as useful energy.

- Motor C uses 30 J of energy and transfers 15 J as useful energy.

   Work in a group to show which motor is the most efficient. Use the space below for your calculations.

Motor _____ is the most efficient because _____

8Kd MANAGING
DISASTERS (STEM)

SB **1** Suggest why portable electricity generators are needed in disaster areas.

....

SB **2a** List the people, equipment and supplies you will need to take to the two villages.

Phi Phi, a small island in Thailand, hot all year round

People	Equipment	Supplies

Lapu, Nepal, cold in the winter, few roads

People	Equipment	Supplies

b Write down *two* differences between your lists for the two countries.

....

....

SB **3a** What is the best way of transporting people and supplies for the disaster in:

Phi Phi ....   Lapu? ....

b Work in your group to write an explanation of why you chose these forms of transport.

....

....

....

4a Write down the *three* most important items to be taken to each place.

Phi Phi ....   Lapu ....

b Work in your group to write an explanation of why you chose these items.

....

8Ke PAYING FOR ENERGY

1 When we use electricity, we have to pay for the energy transferred. Write down the correct unit for each of these quantities used in working out bills.

a time _____ **b** power rating _____ **c** energy used _____

2 A 1 kW electric fire operates for 5 hours.

a How much energy does it use in kilowatt-hours? _____

b Suggest why energy companies do not use joules to measure energy.

_____

3 Calculate the energy used by the following appliances. Use the space on the right to do any working you need to.

a A 2 kW electric fire used for 3 hours.

energy used = _____

b A 0.1 kW light used for 4 hours.

energy used = _____

c A 500 W microwave cooker used for 30 minutes.

500 W = _____ kW

30 minutes = _____ hours

energy used = _____

d A 1500 W hairdryer used for 12 minutes. Energy used = _____

4 Why will using a more efficient appliance help you to use less energy?

_____

_____

5 Mrs Holman is choosing a fridge. Fridge A costs £120 and costs £27 per year to run. Fridge B costs £150 and costs £22 per year to run. Which one should she buy? Explain your answer.

_____

_____

_____

8Ke KEEPING WARM

1a Describe how energy is transferred through solid materials such as metals.

b Describe how energy is transferred through fluids (liquids and gases).

2 What do we mean when we say that one machine is more powerful than another?

3 Look back at your answers to questions **4** and **5** on page 123. Describe what you have learned about in this unit that has helped you to answer questions **1** and **2** on this page better.

SB

4 Describe the difference between:

a energy and temperature

b energy and power.

SB

5a Why is it better to use more efficient appliances?

b How can you calculate the efficiency of an appliance?

1 Ecuador is on the opposite side of the Earth from Malaysia. Explain why it is daytime in Ecuador when it is night time in Malaysia.

....

....

2 Explain how a sundial works. ....

....

3 Explain the difference between mass and weight. Draw a smiley face to show how confident you are in your answer – the bigger the smile, the more confident you are.

4 Draw *one* line from the name of each type of Solar System object to its correct description.

Solar System object	**Description**
asteroid	large, spherical body that orbits the Sun
moon	a body that orbits around a planet
planet	a ball of hot gases in the centre of the Solar System
star	small rocky body that orbits the Sun

5 Some countries, such as New Zealand, have cold winters and warm summers.

In groups, discuss how and why winters and summers are different in this country. Record your group's ideas in the first box below. Ignore the other box for now. There is no right or wrong answer.

Ideas from my group:

What we now think:

1a Tick (✓) the boxes to show which model of the Solar System these statements refer to. Some statements apply to more than one model.

	Ptolemy	**Copernicus**	**Modern**	
i contains five planets	☐	☐	☐	(••)
ii planets orbit around the Sun	☐	☐	☐	(••)
iii Sun orbits around the Earth	☐	☐	☐	(••)
iv planets move in elliptical orbits	☐	☐	☐	(••)
v planets move in circular orbits	☐	☐	☐	(••)
vi the Moon orbits the Earth	☐	☐	☐	(••)

b Draw a smile on the face next to each statement to show how confident you are about your answer—the bigger the smile, the more confident you are.

SB **2** Why did Kepler have more accurate information about the movements of the planets than Ptolemy?

....

....

SB **3** Describe *three* different ways of investigating the planets that were not available to scientists in Kepler's time.

....

....

....

4 Why do scientists today think that the modern model of the Solar System is better than Ptolemy's model?

....

5a Explain how we can see the Moon and the other planets.

....

....

b Look at the diagrams of the Moon. What is this series of shapes called? ....

8La WORKING IN SPACE (STEM)

1 All water on the International Space Station (ISS) is recycled.

a Apply your knowledge of how the human body works to suggest *two* sources of water to be recycled.

....

....

b Explain why the water is recycled.

....

....

2a Most of the renewable resources we use on Earth cannot be used on the Moon. Explain which renewable resources cannot be used on the Moon.

....

....

....

b Explain why using non-renewable resources would be too difficult and expensive on the Moon.

....

....

....

3 Draw your Moon base in the space below. Label the important features.

4 Write a list of the key points you will mention in your presentation.

....

....

1 Label the diagram using words and phrases from the box.

| Equator | North Pole | northern hemisphere | southern hemisphere |

2 Look at the drawing of the Earth.

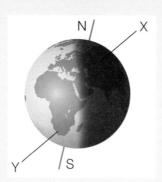

Tick (✓) the boxes to show which statements apply to places X and Y.

	X	Y
a It is daytime.	☐	☐
b It is summer.	☐	☐
c The nights are longer than the days.	☐	☐
d The weather is cold.	☐	☐
e The Sun is high in the sky at midday.	☐	☐
f The days are longer than the nights.	☐	☐
g It is winter.	☐	☐

SB

3 Look at the diagram in question **2**. Describe the difference between summer and winter in place Y in terms of:

a the length of daylight ....

....

b the temperature. ....

4 Look at the diagram in question **2**. Explain why days are longer than nights in summer in place Y.

5 Look at the diagram in question **2**. Explain how the Sun feels at different times of year in place Y. To answer this, tick (✓) *one* box for each of parts **a** and **b**.

a The Sun feels:
- ☐ **A** hotter in summer.
- ☐ **B** hotter in winter.
- ☐ **C** hotter in autumn.
- ☐ **D** the same all year round.

b This is because in the summer:
- ☐ **A** the Earth is closer to the Sun.
- ☐ **B** the Earth is further from the Sun.
- ☐ **C** days are longer than nights.
- ☐ **D** the Sun's rays are more concentrated.

6 If you live near the Equator, the Sun always feels hotter than it does in countries away from the Equator. Add lines and labels to the diagram to help you to explain why.

7 Why does the length of daylight affect the temperature?

SB **1** What is a compass? ....

....

2 Complete these sentences by crossing out the incorrect words.

The north end of a bar magnet will *attract / repel* the north end of another magnet, and *attract / repel* the south end.

A magnetic *compass / field* is the space around a magnet where it has an effect on *all / magnetic* materials. The field is *strongest / weakest* close to the magnet.

You can find the shape of a magnetic field using *copper / iron* filings or a *large / small* compass. The direction of a magnetic field goes from the *north / south* pole to the *north / south* pole of the magnet.

SB **3** Draw the shape of the magnetic field around the bar magnet.

4a Write a check list of things that a good drawing of a magnetic field around a bar magnet should have.

| N | | S |

....

....

....

b Compare your check list and your drawing with others, and write down any way in which you could improve your drawing or your check list.

....

....

5 Two students are talking about compasses.

a What is wrong with statement A?

A Compasses point towards the north magnetic pole because the Earth has a giant bar magnet inside it.

....

....

B Compasses point to the North Pole because the Earth has a magnetic field. The field is shaped as if there is a bar magnet inside the Earth.

....

b What is wrong with statement B? ....

8Ld GRAVITY IN SPACE

1a Tick (✓) the boxes to show if these statements are true or false.

Statement	True	False	
i The force of gravity on an object depends on its mass.	☐	☐	☺
ii On Earth, 'down' is always towards the centre of the Earth.	☐	☐	☺
iii Weight is measured in kilograms.	☐	☐	☺
iv Gravity is the same everywhere in the Solar System.	☐	☐	☺
v Only large objects like the Earth have gravitational fields.	☐	☐	☺
vi Your weight is the force of the Earth's gravity acting on you.	☐	☐	☺

b Draw a smile on the faces to show how confident you are about each answer – the bigger the smile, the more confident you are.

2 Why is a motorbike heavier than a bicycle?

....

3a Add the correct units to the equation for calculating the weight of an object.

weight (_____) = mass (_____) × gravitational field strength (N/kg)

b On Earth, the value of g is 10 N/kg. What does the symbol g stand for?

....

4a Calculate the weight of a 2 kg mass on the Earth.

weight = ... unit ....

b The gravitational field strength on the Moon is 1.6 N/kg. Calculate the weight of the 2 kg mass on the Moon.

weight = ...

8Ld GRAVITY AND ORBITS

1a What stops the Earth from moving away from the Sun?

_____

b What stops the Moon from moving away from the Earth?

_____

2 The diagram shows two planets orbiting a star. The planets are kept in their orbits by the force of gravity between the planets and the star.

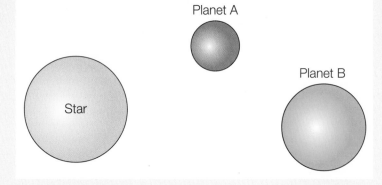

a Give _one_ reason why the greatest force might be between the star and:

i Planet A _____

_____

ii Planet B _____

b Draw arrows on the diagram to show the forces between the star and Planet B.

3 If you climbed to the top of Mount Everest, you would weigh about 1 N less than you do now. Explain why this is so.

_____

_____

4a Explain why the Moon is called a natural satellite of the Earth.

It is a satellite because _____ ,

and it is a natural satellite because _____ .

b Give _two_ uses for artificial satellites.

_____

_____

5 Neptune is about 4.5 billion kilometres from the Sun. Explain how this shows that the Sun's gravitational field extends at least that far.

_____

_____

COMPARISONS (WS)

1 Use your own words to explain what the statement on the right means.

> The ratio of the diameters of Earth and Neptune is 1:4.

2 The gravitational field strength on Mercury is 3.7 N/kg. It is 23.2 N/kg on Jupiter.

a Work in a group to write down how you can work out the ratio of the strength of gravity on Mercury and Jupiter.

b Ask your teacher to check your method. Make any corrections in a different colour.

c Use your method to work out the ratio.

ratio = _____

3 The table shows the length of daylight in June and December in four places in South America.

Place	Day length (hours)		Ratio
	June	**December**	
Buenos Aires, Argentina	9.8	14.5	
Quito, Ecuador	12.1	12.1	
Rio de Janeiro, Brazil	10.7	13.6	
Salvador, Brazil	11.4	12.9	

a Use your method from question **2** to work out the ratio of the day lengths for June and December for each place. Write your answers in the table.

b Write the places in order of their distance from the Equator, starting with Quito.

c Explain your answer to part **b**.

The table shows some information about the planets in our Solar System. Use the information in the table to help you to answer the following questions.

Planet	Diameter (km)	g (N/kg)
Mercury	4880	3.7
Jupiter	142 838	23.2
Saturn	120 412	9.0
Neptune	49 439	11.0

4a Work in a group to write down how to compare two numbers using a:

i fraction converted to a decimal

....

....

ii percentage.

....

....

b Ask your teacher to check your methods. Make any corrections in a different colour.

SB

5 Compare the diameter of Mercury with the diameter of Jupiter using:

a a fraction

b a percentage.

SB

6 Compare the gravitational field strengths of Mercury and Jupiter using:

a a fraction

b a percentage.

SB

7 The diameter of Neptune is only 35 per cent of the diameter of Jupiter. Write this as a decimal.

8 Look at the table on the previous page. Compare the day lengths in June for Buenos Aires and Quito using:

a a fraction

b a percentage.

1 Write the objects in the box in order of size, starting with the smallest.

....

| galaxy | moon | planet | star | Universe |

2 What is a star? ....

3 Write down *two* differences between a star and a planet.

....

....

4 Why does the Sun look much brighter than the other stars?

....

....

5 Why can't we see stars during the day? ....

....

....

6 What is a light year? Tick (✓) *one* box.
☐ **A** The distance light travels from the Sun to the Earth.
☐ **B** The time it takes light to travel from the Sun to the Earth.
☐ **C** The time it takes light to travel from the nearest star to the Earth.
☐ **D** The distance light travels in a year.

7 Explain what the Milky Way is and why we cannot see its shape directly. ....

....

....

8 Share your answer to question **7** with a group. Discuss ways in which you could improve your answers.

Write down *one* improvement you could make to your answer.

....

....

9 Astronomers today can study millions of other galaxies. Explain why modern astronomers know about many more galaxies than observers 200 years ago.

8Le STUDYING SPACE

1a Describe some observations of the planets that can be made from the surface of the Earth.

b Describe *two* ways in which new technology has improved our knowledge of the Solar System.

2a Explain the difference between mass and weight.

b Draw a smile to show your confidence in your answer. The bigger the smile, the more confident you are.

c Look back at your face on page 135. How has your confidence changed since you first answered this question?

3 What is the difference between a natural satellite and an artificial satellite?

4 Some countries, such New Zealand, have cold winters and warm summers.

a In groups, discuss how and why winters and summers are different in these countries. Record your group's ideas in the box at the bottom of page 135.

b How is your new answer different from your original one?

5a The value for *g* on Mars is 3.8 N/kg. Calculate the weight of an 80 kg astronaut on Mars.

weight = _____ unit _____

b The value for *g* on Venus is 8.8 N/kg. Compare the gravitational field strengths of Mars and Venus using a percentage.

COMMAND WORDS

Command word	Meaning
Add/label	Add labels to a diagram or add information to a diagram, table, chart or graph (e.g. adding units to a table).
Calculate	Produce a numerical answer. Remember to show your working.
Circle	Identify a point on a graph or diagram by circling it.
Comment on	See 'Evaluate'.
Complete	Add words to a sentence or add information to a table, graph or diagram.
Deduce	Make a conclusion using the information provided.
Define	Give a brief explanation of what something means.
Describe	Say what something or someone is like or give an account of events.
Design	Plan or invent a way of doing something using your scientific knowledge.
Determine	Select and use numbers from the question (and/or graph) to do a calculation.
Discuss	Identify an issue that is being talked about in the question, and then write about the different aspects of the issue (advantages, disadvantages etc.). You may also need to write an argument in support of or against a particular idea.
Draw	Draw a diagram. Remember that some diagrams will need you to use a ruler (e.g. circuit diagrams).
Estimate	Calculate using rounded or approximate values.
Evaluate	Point out the good/bad points about things and use these points to say whether overall you think things are good or bad.
Explain	Give a reason why something is as it is or how it operates. Use words such as *because* to make clear why things happen.
Give	Write down a simple fact or statement. (Same as 'State' and 'Write down'.)
Give a reason	Give reasons why something is a certain way, including why it operates as it does. Use words such as *because* to make clear why things happen.
Identify	Select some information from a table, chart, graph or text.
List	Write down the steps, terms, etc., that are asked for. No description or explanation is needed. Sometimes the steps need to be given in order.
Name	Write down the name of something.
Outline	State the main points of something (e.g. an argument, a process that involves many steps).

COMMAND WORDS

Plot	Mark points accurately on a grid using data that has been given to you. If you have to draw a chart or graph, remember the points below.
	All charts and graphs need
	• to fill as much of the paper as possible
	• axis lines drawn in
	• divisions on the scales evenly spaced
	• numbers on the scales written in
	• axes labelled
	• units in brackets or with a solidus, after each axis label
	• a title
	• to be plotted accurately
	• to be drawn in (sharp) pencil
	For scatter and line graphs
	• to be plotted with small neat crosses
	• possible line of best fit
	For bar charts:
	• for discontinuous data leave gaps between the bars
	• for grouped continuous data there are no gaps
Predict	Describe an expected result. You can often use 'If …, then …' to make a prediction (e.g. if the air hole on the Bunsen burner is opened wider, then the flame will be hotter).
Sketch	Draw a diagram or graph in freehand. A sketched graph needs a line and labelled axes. The axes do not have scales.
State	Write down a simple fact or statement. (Same as 'Give' and 'Write down'.)
Suggest	Use your scientific knowledge to put forward an idea of your own.
Tick	Add tick (✓) to make a choice.
Use the information	Make use of the data that is given to you in your answer.
Write down	Write down a simple fact or statement. (Same as 'Give' and 'State'.)

THE SI SYSTEM

There is an international standard system of units of measurement, called the **SI system**. All the units in the SI system have defined values. So anyone who uses these units knows that everyone else will understand exactly what the measurement is. The table on the right shows many of these units.

You may find other units for some of these quantities (e.g. inches for length). In science, we always use SI units.

Quantity measured	Name of unit	Symbol
length	metre	m
mass	kilogram	kg
time	second	s
force	newton	N
area	square metres	m^2
volume	cubic metres	m^3
temperature	degrees Celsius	°C
speed	metres per second	m/s
current	ampere or amp	A
energy	joule	J
voltage	volt	V
pressure	pascal	Pa
power	watt	W
frequency	hertz	Hz

Standard prefixes

Sometimes the SI units are not a convenient size, so we use bigger or smaller versions. For instance, it is a bit awkward to measure the thickness of a leaf in metres! It is much easier to use millimetres. An extra part is added to the name of the unit and to its symbol to show we are using a bigger or smaller version. These additions are called **prefixes**.

Prefix	Symbol	Meaning	Example
mega-	M	1 000 000	1 megawatt (1 MW) = 1000 000 W
kilo-	k	1000	1 kilojoule (kJ) = 1000 J
deci-	d	1/10	1 cubic decimetre (dm^3) = 1/1000 m^3 (1/10 m × 1/10 m × 1/10 m)
centi-	c	1/100 (a hundredth)	100 centimetres (cm) = 1 m
milli-	m	1/1000 (a thousandth)	1000 millimetres (mm) = 1 m
micro-	μ	1/1 000 000 (a millionth)	1000 micrometres (μm) = 1 mm
nano-	n	1/1 000 000 000	1 000 000 nanometres (nm) = 1 mm

Other units

There are some units that are still commonly used, which do not fit the standard pattern.

Quantity	Standard unit	Other units still used
time	seconds	minutes, hours, days, years
length	metres	miles
speed	m/s	kilometres per hour (km/h), miles per hour (mph)
volume	m^3	litres (1 litre = 1000 cm^3 = 1 dm^3), millilitres (1 ml = 1 cm^3)

HAZARD SYMBOLS

Many things around a lab have special signs on them warning you of danger. The signs in diamonds below are internationally agreed symbols that you might find on chemicals:

	This symbol warns that a chemical may harm your health if you do not use it properly. The word 'irritant' might be found near this symbol and means that the chemical may give you a rash if you get it on you or make you choke if you breathe it in.

	This symbol tells you that a chemical is corrosive. It will attack your skin if you get it on you.		This symbol tells you that a chemical can cause a serious health problem if you breathe it in (e.g. an allergic reaction, an asthma attack, breathing difficulties).
	This symbol warns you that a chemical is flammable. It catches fire easily.		This symbol warns you that a chemical is oxidising. This means that it can provide a source of oxygen for a fire and make the fire worse.
	This symbol means that a chemical is poisonous (toxic). Poisons can kill.		This symbol warns you that a chemical is very poisonous to water organisms. Chemicals like this should not be released into the environment.

You may also see warning signs like this:

	This is a general warning sign. It may be placed in an area where there is some broken glass or a spilt chemical. Or it may just remind you to be particularly careful when doing something or using particular pieces of equipment or chemicals.

	This symbol means that there is a risk of getting an electric shock.		This 'biohazard' symbol means that there is a certain living thing in an area that may make you ill.

Some symbols tell you to do things so that you stay safe:

	This symbol reminds you to wear safety glasses or goggles when working in a certain area or using particular pieces of equipment or chemicals.		This symbol reminds you to wash your hands after you have done an experiment.

Legend: metal · semi-metal · non-metal

1	2	3	4	5	6	7	8	9	10	11	12	13	14	15	16	17	18
H 1 hydrogen																	He 2 helium
Li 3 lithium	Be 4 beryllium											B 5 boron	C 6 carbon	N 7 nitrogen	O 8 oxygen	F 9 fluorine	Ne 10 neon
Na 11 sodium	Mg 12 magnesium											Al 13 aluminium	Si 14 silicon	P 15 phosphorus	S 16 sulfur	Cl 17 chlorine	Ar 18 argon
K 19 potassium	Ca 20 calcium	Sc 21 scandium	Ti 22 titanium	V 23 vanadium	Cr 24 chromium	Mn 25 manganese	Fe 26 iron	Co 27 cobalt	Ni 28 nickel	Cu 29 copper	Zn 30 zinc	Ga 31 gallium	Ge 32 germanium	As 33 arsenic	Se 34 selenium	Br 35 bromine	Kr 36 krypton
Rb 37 rubidium	Sr 38 strontium	Y 39 yttrium	Zr 40 zirconium	Nb 41 niobium	Mo 42 molybdenum	Tc 43 technetium	Ru 44 ruthenium	Rh 45 rhodium	Pd 46 palladium	Ag 47 silver	Cd 48 cadmium	In 49 indium	Sn 50 tin	Sb 51 antimony	Te 52 tellurium	I 53 iodine	Xe 54 xenon
Cs 55 caesium	Ba 56 barium	La 57 lanthanum	Hf 72 hafnium	Ta 73 tantalum	W 74 tungsten	Re 75 rhenium	Os 76 osmium	Ir 77 iridium	Pt 78 platinum	Au 79 gold	Hg 80 mercury	Tl 81 thallium	Pb 82 lead	Bi 83 bismuth	Po 84 polonium	At 85 astatine	Rn 86 radon
Fr 87 francium	Ra 88 radium	Ac 89 actinium	Rf 104 rutherfordium	Db 105 dubnium	Sg 106 seaborgium	Bh 107 bohrium	Hs 108 hassium	Mt 109 meitnerium	Ds 110 darmstadtium	Rg 111 roentgenium	Cn 112 copernicium	Nh 113 nihonium	Fl 114 flerovium	Mc 115 moscovium	Lv 116 livermorium	Ts 117 tennessine	Og 118 oganesson

Lanthanides:

Ce 58 cerium	Pr 59 praseodymium	Nd 60 neodymium	Pm 61 promethium	Sm 62 samarium	Eu 63 europium	Gd 64 gadolinium	Tb 65 terbium	Dy 66 dysprosium	Ho 67 holmium	Er 68 erbium	Tm 69 thulium	Yb 70 ytterbium	Lu 71 lutetium

Actinides:

Th 90 thorium	Pa 91 protactinium	U 92 uranium	Np 93 neptunium	Pu 94 plutonium	Am 95 americium	Cm 96 curium	Bk 97 berkelium	Cf 98 californium	Es 99 einsteinium	Fm 100 fermium	Md 101 mendelevium	No 102 nobelium	Lr 103 lawrencium

Title:	Anotomical 3D KS3 Science uJ	
Client:	KJA	Font: Arial reg. 11/13pt
Date:	2 Dec 2013	Rev: 16 Dec 2013
		18 Dec 2013

Published by Pearson Education Limited, 80 Strand, London, WC2R 0RL.

www.pearsonschools.co.uk

Text © Pearson Education Limited 2019
Writers: Mark Levesley, Sue Kearsey, Ian Bradley, Alice Jensen, Sarah Longshaw, Kat Day, Penny Johnson
Series editor: Mark Levesley
Edited by Just Content
Typeset by PDQ Digital Media Solutions Ltd.
Original illustrations © Pearson Education Limited 2019
Cover photo © Miroslav Hlavko/Shutterstock

The rights of Mark Levesley, Sue Kearsey, Ian Bradley, Alice Jensen, Sarah Longshaw, Kat Day, Penny Johnson to be identified as authors of this work have been asserted by them in accordance with the Copyright, Designs and Patents Act 1988.

First published 2019

22 21 20 19
10 9 8 7 6 5 4 3

British Library Cataloguing in Publication Data
A catalogue record for this book is available from the British Library

ISBN 978 1292 9414 8

Printed in Italy by L.E.G.O S.p.A

Note from the publisher
Pearson has robust editorial processes, including answer and fact checks, to ensure the accuracy of the content in this publication, and every effort is made to ensure this publication is free of errors. We are, however, only human, and occasionally errors do occur. Pearson is not liable for any misunderstandings that arise as a result of errors in this publication, but it is our priority to ensure that the content is accurate. If you spot an error, please do contact us at resourcescorrections@pearson.com so we can make sure it is corrected.